Geography
Revision

Adam Arnell

Contents

Page

4–5	A curious letter	The local area
6–7	Important places	Human features of the British Isles
8–9	The ups and downs of the British Isles	Physical features of the British Isles
10–11	Test your knowledge 1	
12–13	Izzy investigates	Research skills
14–15	The whole world in your hands	Using an atlas
16–17	Where am I?	Longitude and latitude
18–19	Test your knowledge 2	
20–21	The secret agent	Four-figure grid references
22–23	The mystery deepens	Six-figure grid references
24–25	Which way now?	Distance and direction
26–27	Test your knowledge 3	
28–29	An Englishman's home...	Housing development
30–31	Who would live in a place like this?	Settlement sites
32–33	Everybody's going through changes	Land use in urban areas
34–35	Test your knowledge 4	
36–37	How others see us	Perceptions of Britain
38–39	Who are the British?	The people of Britain
40–41	Wherever you lay your hat...	Migration
42–43	Test your knowledge 5	

44–45	Six billion and counting	Global population growth
46–47	Where are all the babies?	Population growth rates
48–49	An uneven world	Population distribution
50–51	Test your knowledge 6	
52–53	Flood alert	Effects of flooding in the UK
54–55	After the flood	Causes of flooding in the UK
56–57	Holding back the water	Flood control
58–59	Test your knowledge 7	
60–61	Flood disaster in Bangladesh	Effects of flooding in Bangladesh
62–63	Why are there floods?	Causes of flooding in Bangladesh
64–65	It's a hazardous world	Natural hazards
66–67	Test your knowledge 8	
68–69	The Olympics	Location of the Olympics
70–71	Olympic winners and losers	Benefits and problems of the Olympics
72–73	'A journey of a thousand miles begins with a single step' (Chinese proverb)	Planning a journey
74–75	Test your knowledge 9	
76–77	Glossary	
78–80	Answers	

A curious letter

As the sun rose over England, a letter addressed to Izzy Witherbottom landed on the doormat of a large house in north Oxford. Later, as Izzy and her father, Sir Ralph Witherbottom, were eating their breakfast in the dining room, Max the butler appeared.

'Good morning, Max,' said Ralph. 'What have you there?'

'A most curiously addressed letter for Izzy,' he replied.

'Oh, let me see,' cried Izzy excitedly.

Max handed Izzy the letter and she studied it closely. It had an unfamiliar stamp, and it certainly was addressed in a curious manner.

> Miss Izzy Witherbottom
> 24 Blenheim Gardens
> Oxford
> Oxfordshire
> England
> Great Britain
> United Kingdom
> British Isles
> Europe
> The world

'I wonder who it's from?' said Izzy, as she carefully opened the envelope and took out a letter. 'Oh, it's from Abdul, my new pen-pal in Bangladesh.'

Ralph looked over the top of his newspaper. 'You will have to write back and tell him that he needn't write such a complicated address. Just "England" will do.'

'Uh-hum,' coughed Max. 'That's true, but he is absolutely correct that England is part of <u>Great Britain</u>, which is part of the <u>United Kingdom</u>, which is part of the <u>British Isles</u>, which is part of the continent of <u>Europe</u>. Now, I wonder how many young people in this country know that!' Max glanced knowingly in the direction of Izzy.

Izzy, who was engrossed in reading her letter, thought it best if she pretended not to have heard Max's comment – especially since she hadn't known it!

So that means I'm English, British, and Europe-ish.

I think the word you're looking for is "European."

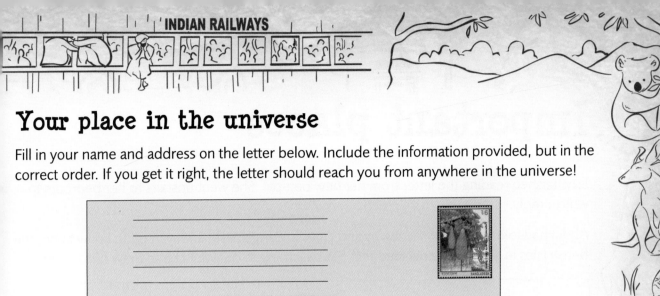

Your place in the universe

Fill in your name and address on the letter below. Include the information provided, but in the correct order. If you get it right, the letter should reach you from anywhere in the universe!

| Your country | Your street | United Kingdom | Great Britain |

| Your house number or name | British Isles | The universe | The world |

| Your name | Your county | Your village, town or city | Europe |

• TOP TIPS •

Writing to a pen-pal (or emailing them) can be a great way to learn about another region, or even another country. It is best to make contact through someone you already know and trust. Try asking your teachers if they can recommend anyone – your school may already have links with schools in other countries.

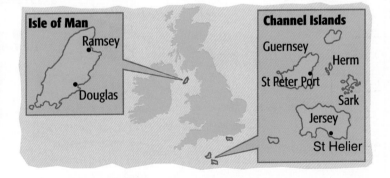

Isle of Man
Ramsey
Douglas

Channel Islands
Guernsey
Herm
St Peter Port
Sark
Jersey
St Helier

DID YOU KNOW?

• Great Britain includes England, Scotland and Wales.

• The United Kingdom includes England, Scotland, Wales and Northern Ireland.

• The British Isles includes England, Scotland, Wales, Northern Ireland, the Republic of Ireland, the Isle of Man and the Channel Islands.

Important places

Izzy finished reading the letter from her new pen-pal. She went upstairs to her bedroom to write a reply.

Abdul had told Izzy about the towns and cities in Bangladesh, and wanted to know about the British Isles in return. She decided that the best thing to do would be to draw him a map.

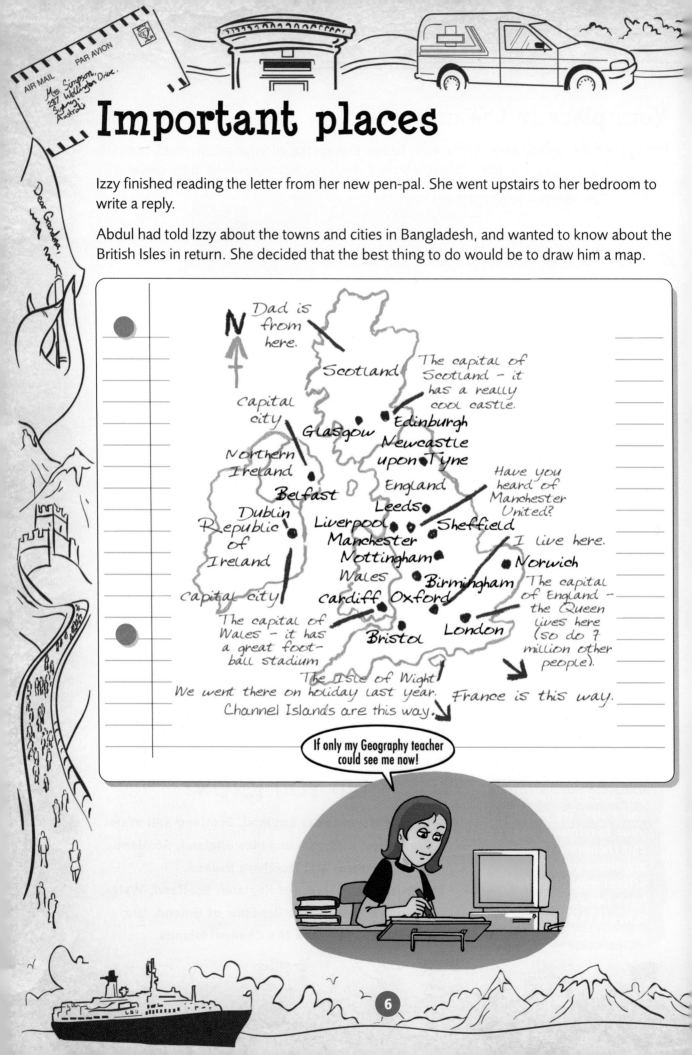

The great cycle race

Ralph is taking part in a cycle race around the British Isles. Look at the map. The race begins in London and then goes to 12 other cities.

Fill in the table below. It needs to show the 12 cities in the race in the correct order.

Start	London
City 1	
City 2	
City 3	
City 4	
City 5	
City 6	
City 7	
City 8	
City 9	
City 10	
City 11	
City 12	

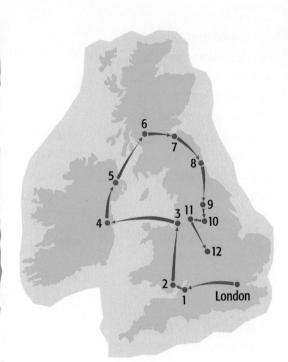

DID YOU KNOW?

The United Kingdom is part of the <u>European Union</u>, an organisation of 25 countries: Austria, Belgium, Cyprus, Czech Republic, Denmark, Estonia, Finland, France, Germany, Greece, Hungary, Ireland, Italy, Latvia, Lithuania, Luxemburg, Malta, The Netherlands, Poland, Portugal, Slovakia, Slovenia, Spain, Sweden, United Kingdom.

• TOP TIPS •

The 10 biggest cities in the British Isles, in order, are:
• London
• Birmingham
• Leeds
• Glasgow
• Sheffield
• Bradford
• Liverpool
• Edinburgh
• Manchester
• Bristol

The ups and downs of the British Isles

Two weeks later, Izzy received a postcard from Abdul. On the front of the postcard was a map of Bangladesh, and on the back Abdul had described the physical geography of his country.

Abdul wrote that Bangladesh was very flat, apart from one area called the Chittagong Hills, and that there were many big rivers, such as the Brahmaputra and the Ganges. Abdul added that he would like to visit the British Isles as he had heard that it was very hilly and he would love to explore such an interesting landscape.

Later that day, Izzy made her own postcard and drew a map of the British Isles on the front. She used her geography textbook to add some notes about the physical geography that she thought Abdul would find interesting.

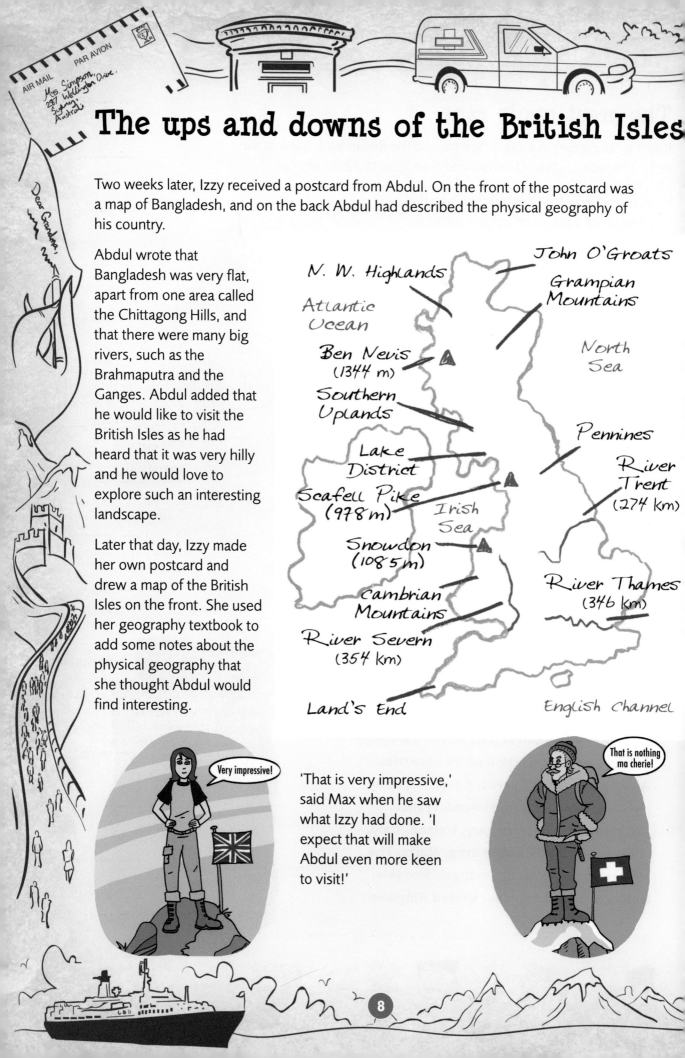

N. W. Highlands

Atlantic Ocean

Ben Nevis (1344 m)

Southern Uplands

Lake District

Scafell Pike (978 m)

Snowdon (1085 m)

Cambrian Mountains

River Severn (354 km)

Land's End

John O'Groats

Grampian Mountains

North Sea

Pennines

River Trent (274 km)

Irish Sea

River Thames (346 km)

English Channel

Very impressive!

'That is very impressive,' said Max when he saw what Izzy had done. 'I expect that will make Abdul even more keen to visit!'

That is nothing ma cherie!

8

The confused tourist

Help the confused tourist by joining the statements about the British Isles on the left with the correct information on the right. The first one has been done for you.

Mountains in England	Ben Nevis
The highest mountain in England	Snowdon
Mountains in Wales	220 miles
The highest mountain in Wales	Cambrian Mountains
Mountains in Scotland	Land's End
The highest mountain in Scotland	John O'Groats
The length of the River Thames	Pennines
The length of the River Trent	170 miles
The length of the River Severn	215 miles
The most northerly point	Grampian Mountains
The most southerly point	Scafell Pike

DID YOU KNOW?

- The total land area of the UK is 244 820 km².
- The UK has over 12 000 miles of coastline.
- The UK has over 5000 rivers.
- The highest point in the UK is Ben Nevis at 1344 m.
- The lowest point in the UK is the Fens at −4 m.
- It is 874 miles from John O'Groats to Land's End.

• TOP TIPS •

- The rocks in the north and west of Britain are older and more resistant to <u>erosion</u>. This means that the landscape is more mountainous, with steep hills and valleys.

- The rocks in the south and east of Britain are younger and worn away more easily, resulting in gently rolling hills and flat plains.

Test your knowledge 1

1 Match the maps with the correct titles.

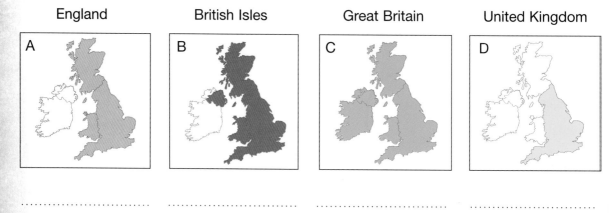

England   British Isles   Great Britain   United Kingdom

A   B   C   D

....

(4 marks)

2 Name the cities that are shown on the map.

F_____

G_____

H_____

E_____

I_____

J_____

D_____

K_____

L_____

B_____

A_____

C_____

(12 marks)

3 Arrange the following cities in order of size from largest to smallest.

Glasgow ....

Edinburgh ....

Liverpool ....

London ....

Birmingham ....

Sheffield ....

Manchester ....

Leeds ....

Bradford ....

Bristol ....

(10 marks)

4 Odd one out.
Which countries in the following lists are not members of the European Union?
Underline your chosen countries.

a) United Kingdom, Spain, Switzerland, Greece, Latvia

b) France, Russia, Austria, Hungary, Ireland

c) Sweden, Slovakia, Portugal, Turkey, Germany

d) Slovenia, Iceland, Malta, Cyprus, Estonia

e) Luxemburg, Netherlands, Belgium, Denmark, Egypt

(5 marks)

5 Which of the following statements are true and which are false?

a) The tallest mountain in England is Mount Snowdon. ....

b) The tallest mountain in the UK is Ben Nevis. ....

c) The longest river in the UK is the Severn. ....

d) The River Thames is 750 miles long. ....

e) The most southerly point of the UK is John O'Groats. ....

f) The UK has over 12 000 miles of coastline. ....

g) Northwest Britain is mountainous. ....

h) The UK has over 10 000 rivers. ....

(8 marks)

(Total 39 marks)

Izzy investigates

Izzy arrived home from school with a worried look on her face.

'What's up?' asked her dad.

'Oh, nothing,' replied Izzy. 'It's just that I have to write a project on a foreign country by Monday, and I don't know where to start.'

'Why not write about Bangladesh?' said Ralph. 'You've already learnt quite a lot from your pen-pal Abdul.'

'That's a great idea,' she said cheering up a bit. 'I'll start straight away.'

Izzy began by thinking about the topics she wanted to research. She decided to write about:

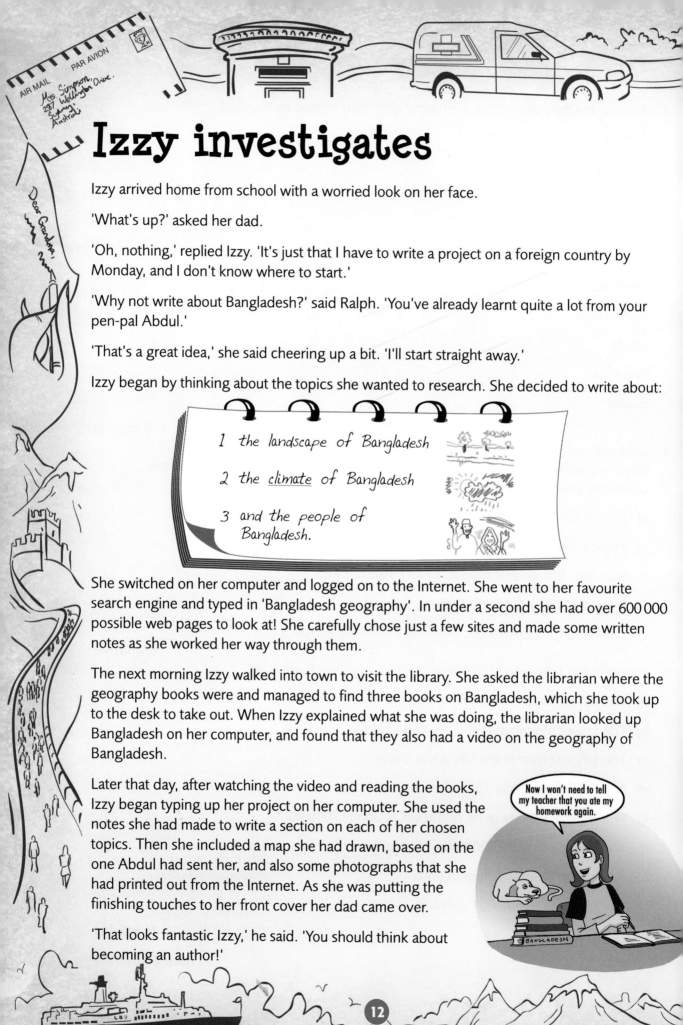

1 the landscape of Bangladesh

2 the <u>climate</u> of Bangladesh

3 and the people of Bangladesh.

She switched on her computer and logged on to the Internet. She went to her favourite search engine and typed in 'Bangladesh geography'. In under a second she had over 600 000 possible web pages to look at! She carefully chose just a few sites and made some written notes as she worked her way through them.

The next morning Izzy walked into town to visit the library. She asked the librarian where the geography books were and managed to find three books on Bangladesh, which she took up to the desk to take out. When Izzy explained what she was doing, the librarian looked up Bangladesh on her computer, and found that they also had a video on the geography of Bangladesh.

Later that day, after watching the video and reading the books, Izzy began typing up her project on her computer. She used the notes she had made to write a section on each of her chosen topics. Then she included a map she had drawn, based on the one Abdul had sent her, and also some photographs that she had printed out from the Internet. As she was putting the finishing touches to her front cover her dad came over.

Now I won't need to tell my teacher that you ate my homework again.

'That looks fantastic Izzy,' he said. 'You should think about becoming an author!'

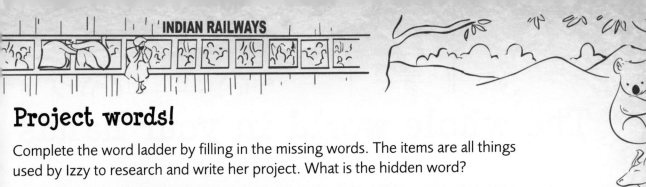

Project words!

Complete the word ladder by filling in the missing words. The items are all things used by Izzy to research and write her project. What is the hidden word?

1.
2.
3.
4.
5.
6.
7.
8.

DID YOU KNOW?

The Internet is a fantastic source of information, but with over 8 billion web pages it can be difficult to find exactly what you are looking for. The more key words you can include in your search the better. For example, typing the words:

`Bangladesh geography climate`

will find more relevant sites than just typing 'Bangladesh'. Most search engines ignore common words such as 'where', 'how', 'the', 'of'. However, if you want to include them in your search, put your key words in quotation marks:

`"the climate of Bangladesh"`

Happy surfing!

• TOP TIPS •

• **When researching a topic, especially if you are using the Internet, you need to evaluate the information.**

  – **Who wrote it?**
  – **Is the information reliable?**
  – **Is the information up to date?**
  – **Is the information biased (one-sided)?**

• **Downloading information and photographs from a website can help to make your work really good, but make sure that you re-write any text in your own words, and include the names of the websites that you used.**

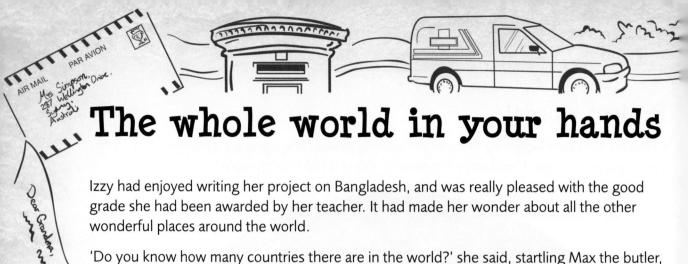

The whole world in your hands

Izzy had enjoyed writing her project on Bangladesh, and was really pleased with the good grade she had been awarded by her teacher. It had made her wonder about all the other wonderful places around the world.

'Do you know how many countries there are in the world?' she said, startling Max the butler, who was busy polishing the goldfish bowl.

'Good question, Izzy. I'm not sure. But I know how we can find out,' replied Max.

Together they went to Ralph's private library, where Max pulled a large book off the shelf.

'This <u>atlas</u> should answer your question,' he said.

Izzy opened the atlas at a map of the world. She began counting all the countries, each of which was a different colour, but soon lost count. Although she tried several times, she found it completely impossible to count them accurately.

Frustrated, Izzy began flicking through the atlas and was surprised to discover that it contained much more than just maps of countries. She found maps that showed mountains, plains, seas, lakes, rivers, roads and railways. She pored over maps of geology, temperature, rainfall, vegetation, agriculture and industry. She lost herself in lists of population, birth rates, death rates and life expectancy, and before she knew it, it was time for tea.

CHINA

That's where I'm from.

'Did you find the answer to your question?' asked Max, as he expertly sliced the top off Izzy's boiled egg.

'Yes, thank you,' replied Izzy. 'I found a table in the atlas, and it turns out there are a total of 193 countries in the world.' She paused for a moment and then added, 'Wouldn't it be amazing to visit them all.'

Name that country!

Identify the countries shown below.

Use this list to help you. The country names have been scrambled:

AUS   ATRAILAUS   PANJA   KU   NAICH   TAILY   DIANI

Note: the shapes are correct but they are not to scale.

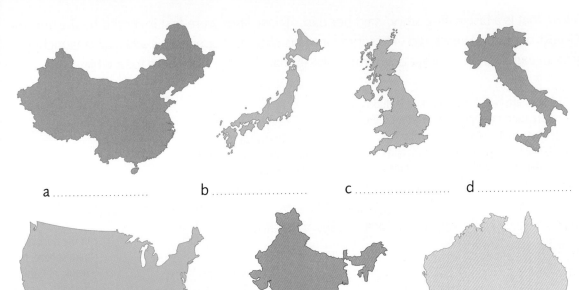

a ....   b ....   c ....   d ....

e ....   f ....   g ....

DID YOU KNOW?

A collection of maps in a book was first called an 'atlas' by Gerard Mercator (famous map maker) in 1578, in honour of the mythical Greek god Atlas. Atlas fought against the king of the gods, Zeus, but lost, and was given the punishment of holding the world above his head. Pictures of Atlas appeared on the front of early atlases.

· TOP TIPS ·

There are two ways of finding information in an atlas.

1   The contents page at the front gives details about what is on each page. This is particularly useful for finding maps of whole regions.
2   The index, at the back of the atlas, is best for looking up countries, cities and towns. Usually the index will tell you the page number and a grid reference to help you find the place.

Where am I?

While looking in her father's atlas, Izzy noticed that the maps were criss-crossed by lots of thin blue lines. When she next had the chance she asked him about them.

'Now, that is a fascinating story,' said her dad. 'Those lines were first invented by the ancient Greeks over 2000 years ago.' He settled into his chair and opened his atlas as he launched into an explanation. Izzy sat down too, fearing that she might be there for a while.

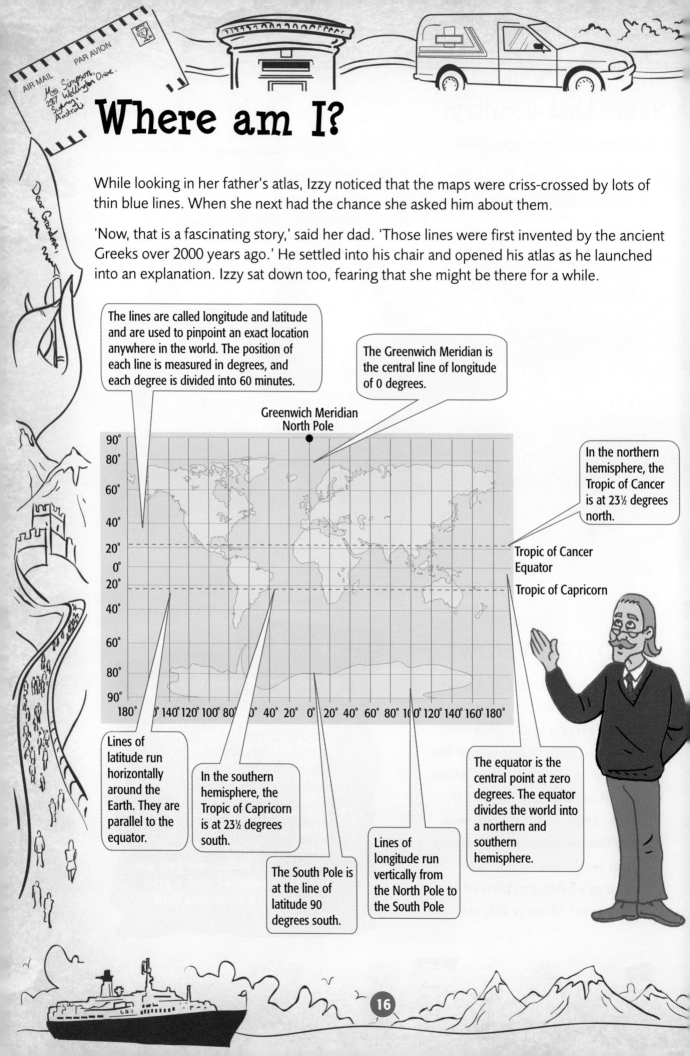

The lines are called longitude and latitude and are used to pinpoint an exact location anywhere in the world. The position of each line is measured in degrees, and each degree is divided into 60 minutes.

The Greenwich Meridian is the central line of longitude of 0 degrees.

In the northern hemisphere, the Tropic of Cancer is at 23½ degrees north.

Lines of latitude run horizontally around the Earth. They are parallel to the equator.

In the southern hemisphere, the Tropic of Capricorn is at 23½ degrees south.

The South Pole is at the line of latitude 90 degrees south.

Lines of longitude run vertically from the North Pole to the South Pole

The equator is the central point at zero degrees. The equator divides the world into a northern and southern hemisphere.

Greenwich Meridian
North Pole

Tropic of Cancer
Equator

Tropic of Capricorn

World cruise

Use the longitude and latitude co-ordinates below to navigate a cruise ship safely on its journey around the world. Plot the position of the ship on the map and join the points with a straight line. Where is the cruise ship's final destination?

Start	51°N 1°E
Position 1	20°N 20°W
Position 2	20°S 20°W
Position 3	40°S 20°E
Position 4	20°S 60°E
Position 5	0° 80°E
Position 6	20°N 120°E
Position 7	0° 140°E
Position 8	0° 140°W
Finish	33°N 118°W

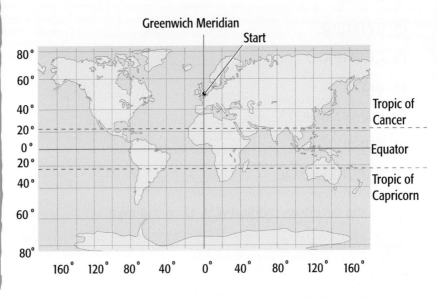

Final destination ....

DID YOU KNOW?

1 The first person to think of using grid lines on a map was a Greek astronomer called Hipparchus who lived 2300 years ago.

2 In AD150, another Greek scientist, called Ptolemy, used lines of longitude and latitude on his maps in his book on geography.

3 The position of the lines as they are today was finally agreed at an international conference in 1884.

• TOP TIPS •

• It is important to get latitude and longitude the right way round. To remember latitude, imagine the lines as the horizontal rungs of a ladder, and think of the word 'ladder-tude'.

Test your knowledge 2

1 Re-arrange the letters to identify words that are connected with doing research.

a) LRABRYI   _ _ _ _ _ _ _

b) NTOES   _ _ _ _ _

c) IRNTTENE   _ _ _ _ _ _ _ _

d) CEOMPRTU   _ _ _ _ _ _ _ _

e) BKOO   _ _ _ _

f) PGHROAPHOTS   _ _ _ _ _ _ _ _ _ _

g) VOEID   _ _ _ _ _

h) SARCHEEINNGE   _ _ _ _ _ _ / _ _ _ _ _ _

(8 marks)

2 Name the countries marked A to G on the map.

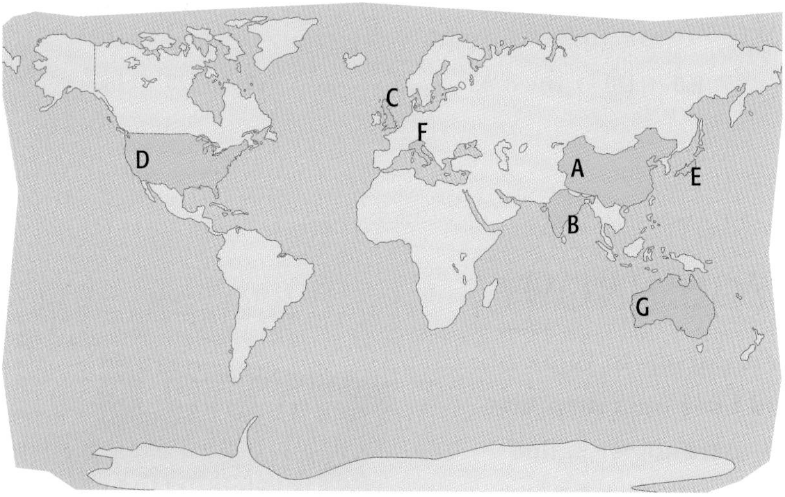

A ....

B ....

C ....

D ....

E ....

F ....

G ....

(7 marks)

3 Label the globe using the words below to help you.

Greenwich Meridian	Tropic of Capricorn	
Tropic of Cancer	South Pole	North Pole
Equator		

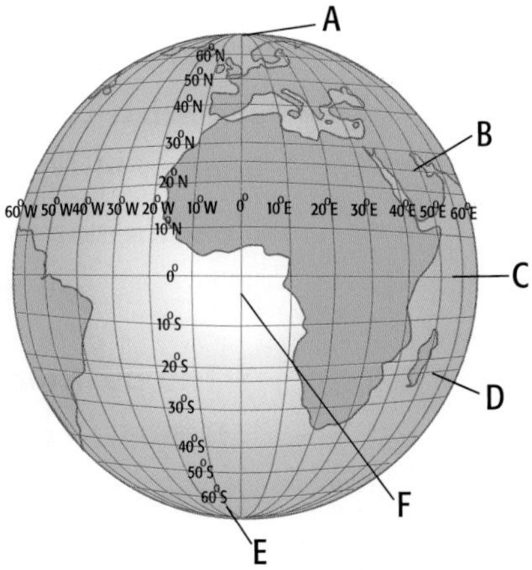

A ....   D ....

B ....   E ....

C ....   F ....

(6 marks)

4 Name the continent found at the following locations.

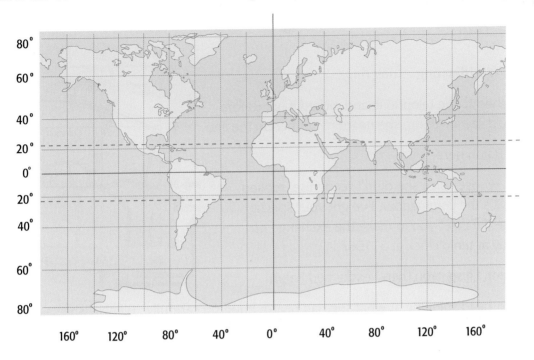

Latitude	Longitude	Continent
a) 40°N	100°W	
b) 40°N	100°E	
c) 50°N	20°E	
d) 80°S	20°E	
e) 20°S	60°W	
f) 20°S	140°E	
g) 0°	20°E	

(7 marks)

(Total 28 marks)

The secret agent

'Ring ring ... ring ring ... ring ring ...'

Izzy rushed to the telephone and picked it up. Before she could say anything, she heard her father on the line.

'Hello, Ralph here.'

A man, whose voice she didn't recognise, replied, 'Ralph, it's the commander. I've got your special package. I'll meet you to make the exchange on Saturday at ten o'clock at 511067.'

'Excellent, I'll see you then,' exclaimed Ralph.

Izzy, her head spinning at what she had heard, hung up carefully. 'Blimey,' she said to Spotless, who was busy chewing a slipper. 'I think Dad might be a secret agent!'

Izzy decided to investigate. She quickly noted down the code and went to find Max, who was making pizzas for tea.

'Max, do you have any idea what this stands for?' asked Izzy showing him her scrap of paper. 'Mmmm,' pondered Max, stretching out the pizza dough and spinning it skilfully above his head. 'It looks to me like an <u>Ordnance Survey</u> grid reference. Why do you need to know?' 'Oh, just some homework,' replied Izzy, scurrying off to investigate further.

Izzy logged on to the Ordnance Survey website, where she began by learning how <u>four-figure grid references</u> work. She discovered that OS maps are criss-crossed by thin blue lines that divide Britain into thousands of 1 km by 1 km squares. The lines running up and down the map are called <u>eastings</u> and the lines running across the map are called <u>northings</u>. A four-figure grid reference is made up of the number for the easting, followed by the number for the northing.

I always wondered exactly what Dad did for a living!

Izzy rummaged through her desk until she found a map of Oxfordshire. She placed one finger on '51' at the bottom of the map, and another finger on '06' up the side of the map. Slowly she moved her fingers towards each other, until finally they met in central Oxford. Suddenly, Ralph appeared, making Izzy jump.

'Didn't you hear me?' said Ralph innocently. 'Come and eat your "quattro formaggi" while it's still hot!'

Crack the code

Use the four-figure grid references below to crack the secret code. The first letter has been done for you.

1. ~~13 20~~, 14 22, 13 24

2. 11 21, 10 22, 11 24, 12 23

3. 10 23, 10 24, 13 22, 13 22, 11 21

4. 14 22, 13 24, 10 24, 14 23, 11 23, 13 22, 12 21

5. 11 23, 10 22

6. 10 20, 11 24, 11 21, 11 20, 11 24, 12 23

	10	11	12	13	14	15
25	A	O	B	E	D	
24	F	I	W	G	V	
23	N	I	J	L	H	
22	K	S	Y	P	Q	
21	M	C	R	T	U	
20						

Answer: T ....
....
....

• TOP TIPS •

• **Four-figure grid references are quite straightforward, but you need to remember which corner of the grid square to use. It is always the bottom left-hand corner, known as 'VIC', for 'Very Important Corner'.**

Where is grid reference 02 22?

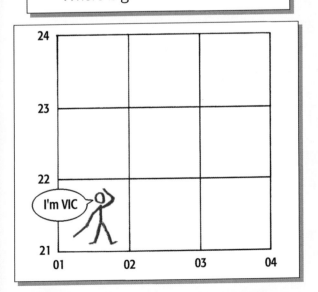

DID YOU KNOW?

The Ordnance Survey began mapping Britain in 1791. It was given the job of producing maps for the army, to make sure that Britain could defend itself in case it was attacked. It took 20 years to map one third of Britain and Wales.

The mystery deepens

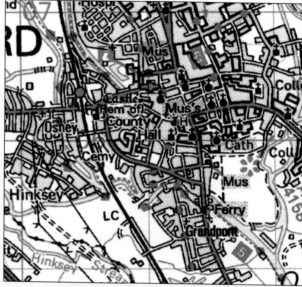

Izzy wolfed down her tea so she could get back to her map, and work out exactly where her father was meeting the mysterious 'commander'.

The grid reference she had overheard was 511067. Izzy had already worked out the four-figure grid reference, and knew that the meeting was taking place somewhere in the centre of Oxford, but she needed to know the exact spot. She logged on to the Ordnance Survey website again, and found a section on how to use six-figure grid references.

'Move a pencil along the bottom of the map until you come to the line with the first two numbers of the grid reference,' Izzy read to herself, resting her pencil on the '51' line. 'To find the third number imagine that the distance to the next gridline is divided into ten small parts, and then move your pencil until you come to about the right place.' Izzy slid her pencil to the right, where she imagined the number '1' would be.

'Move another pencil up the side of the map, until you come to the line with the fourth and fifth numbers of the grid reference.' Izzy did so, moving a second pencil to the '06' line. 'To find the sixth number, again imagine the distance to the next gridline is divided into ten small parts. Move the pencil upwards until you come to the right place.' Izzy carefully guided her pencil upwards and stopped where she thought the number '7' would be. Now, excitedly, she slowly slid the pencils towards each other, until finally they met at 511067.

I'm sure I buried it at 641278.

Izzy peered closely at the map. 'The place at 511067 is called "Mus"! What on earth is a "Mus"?' She slumped into her seat, as she realised that her detective work was not yet over.

Dot to dot

Mark each six-figure grid reference on to the grid with a small dot.
Join them together carefully in the right order. What do you see?

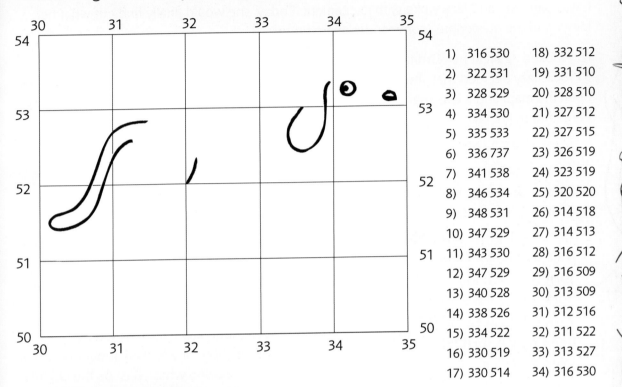

1) 316 530	18) 332 512
2) 322 531	19) 331 510
3) 328 529	20) 328 510
4) 334 530	21) 327 512
5) 335 533	22) 327 515
6) 336 737	23) 326 519
7) 341 538	24) 323 519
8) 346 534	25) 320 520
9) 348 531	26) 314 518
10) 347 529	27) 314 513
11) 343 530	28) 316 512
12) 347 529	29) 316 509
13) 340 528	30) 313 509
14) 338 526	31) 312 516
15) 334 522	32) 311 522
16) 330 519	33) 313 527
17) 330 514	34) 316 530

• TOP TIPS •

- **It is easy to remember the correct order for writing grid references.**

- **The number along the bottom of the map comes first, followed by the number up the side.**

- **The following well-known saying may help you remember this: 'Along the corridor, and up the stairs.'**

DID YOU KNOW?

The National Grid system was introduced in 1935, allowing any point in Britain to be accurately pinpointed for the first time. This was aided by building a network of 'triangulation pillars' (concrete pillars about four feet high) which were used to work out the exact shape of the country by using trigonometry.

Which way now?

It was Saturday and Izzy woke with excitement. Today, she would finally find out what her father and the mysterious 'commander' were up to.

Izzy looked again at her Ordnance Survey map, and quickly found the grid reference 511067. Izzy decided that she might draw attention to herself if she had to keep stopping to open the map, and it was therefore best to write herself some directions, avoiding the route her father might take.

Leave house.

Head south-east along Blenheim Gardens for 400 metres.

Turn right onto Woodstock road and walk south for 1 km.

Turn left into Moreton Road, head north-east for 250 metres.

Turn right on to Banbury Road and head south for 1.5 km until the road joins St Giles.

Head south for another 250 metres.

The meeting point will be on the right.

Izzy left the house very quietly and began walking into the city. After a while she became aware that she was being followed. She turned quickly ...

... to see Spotless bounding towards her. 'Oh, Spotless,' she said. 'What am I going to do with you? I suppose you had better come with me now!'

One hour later, Izzy reached her destination. She looked about her and at once realised what 'Mus' on the OS map stood for. 'Of course! It's the Ashmolean Museum,' she said to Spotless. Spotless barked and ran towards the museum. Without thinking, Izzy ran through the gates after him, and bumped straight into her father.

'Izzy!' 'Dad!' They said in unison.

'What are you doing here, Izzy?' said Ralph.

'Um ... I have some homework on Roman Britain,' replied Izzy, thinking quickly.

'Really,' replied Ralph. 'You must come and meet my friend Commander Dick Brown. He is an expert on the Romans. We are meeting here, actually. He has a rare Roman coin I'd like to add to my collection. I'm sure he'd be happy to answer all of your questions!'

'Errr ... that's great,' said Izzy, unconvincingly. Suddenly she felt very, very, foolish.

North, east, south, west, north, east, south, west! My tail keeps changing direction!

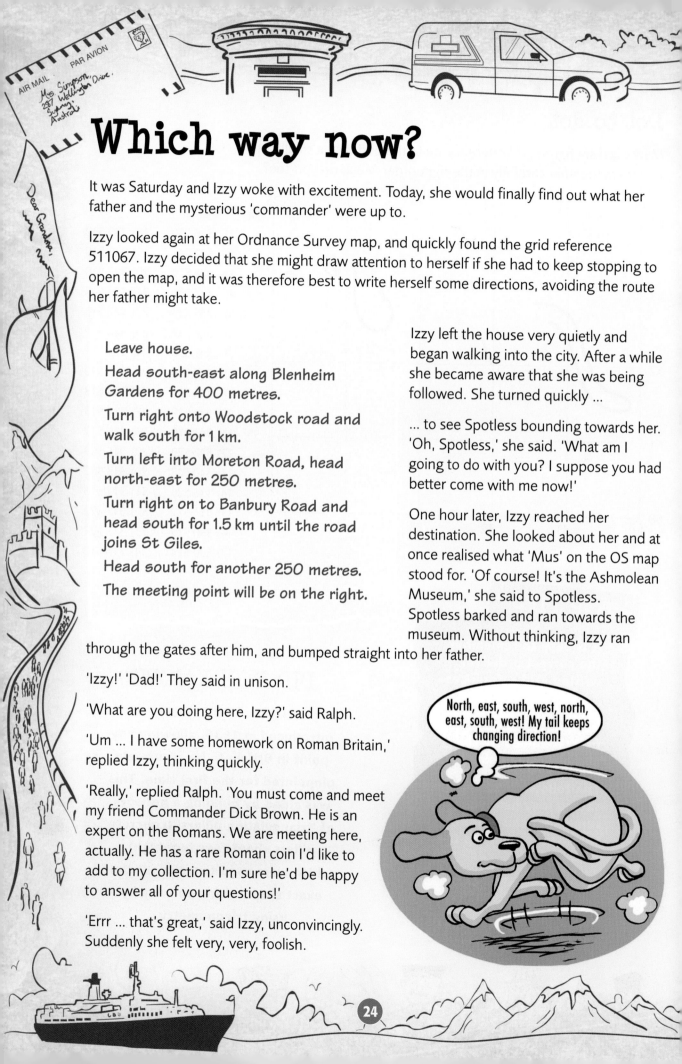

Yo ho ho ho! A pirate's life for me!

You have found an ancient map and some directions. They will lead you to the buried treasure of Purplebeard the pirate. Follow the directions (mark on your route with a pencil) to find exactly where it is.

Directions

Leave the ship and go onshore.

Go west for 1km.

Go north west for 1km.

Go north for 1km.

Go east for 2km.

Go south east for 1km.

Where are you?

Mark the spot with a skull and cross-bones.

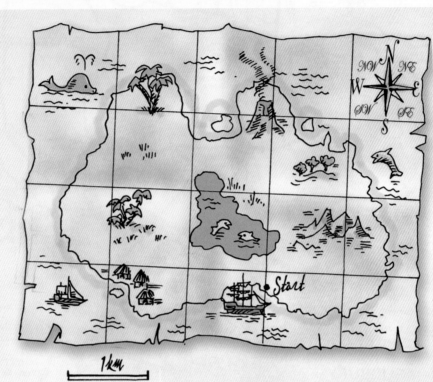

1km

DID YOU KNOW?

- **Maps are produced at different <u>scales</u>.**
- **The most commonly used map scale is 1 : 50 000. This means that the map covers an area 50 000 times smaller than the real life area. So 2 centimetres are equal to 1 kilometre.**
- **On a 1 : 25 000 map, 4 centimetres equal 1 kilometre. So a 1 : 25 000 map is twice as detailed as a 1 : 50 000 map.**
- **If this seems confusing, don't worry! All you need to remember is that, whatever the scale of the map, one grid square always equals one kilometre.**

• TOP TIPS •

- **Ordnance Survey maps always have compass directions on them.**

- **It is easy to remember that north is always at the top of the map.**

- **To remember the order of all the compass directions (north, east, south, west), think of the phrase:**

  'Naughty Elephants Squirt Water'.

Test your knowledge 3

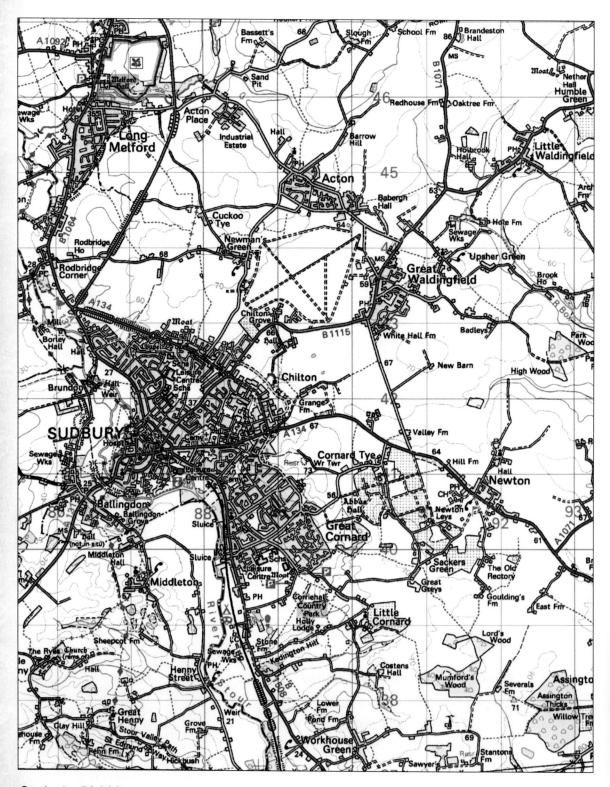

Scale 1 : 50 000

1   What are the names of the settlements at the following four-figure grid references?

   a) 87 39 ....

   b) 90 43 ....

   c) 86 40 ....

(3 marks)

2   What are the four-figure grid references for the following settlements?

   a) Long Melford ....

   b) Little Waldingfield ....

   c) Acton ....

(3 marks)

3 What symbols are found at the following six-figure grid references?

   a) 912 439 ....

   b) 883 392 ....

   c) 885 438 ....

(3 marks)

4   What is the six-figure grid reference for the following?

   a) The train station in Sudbury ━━●━━

   b) The golf course next to Newton ⚑

   c) The public house in Acton PH

(3 marks)

5   What is the direction between the following places?

   a) Newton to Little Waldingfield ....

   b) Little Waldingfield to Long Melford ....

   c) Long Melford to Great Waldingfield ....

(3 marks)

6   What is the straight line distance between the following places?

   a) The church in Acton and the church in Little Waldingfield

   ....

   b) The church in Middleton and the church in Newton

   ....

   c) The church in Newton and the church in Acton

   ....

(3 marks)

(Total 18 marks)

An Englishman's home...

Peace reigned in the Witherbottom household. Izzy was watching the television, Max was mowing the lawn, Ralph was reading the newspaper, and Spotless was dozing and dreaming of rabbits. Without warning, the peace was shattered by a cry from Ralph.

'Good grief ... I don't believe it!'

The members of the family came running.

'What is it?' enquired Max.

'What's up, Dad?' asked Izzy.

'Woof!' barked Spotless, not wanting to be left out.

Ralph replied, 'It says here in the newspaper that they are going to build a new housing estate on the meadow next to our house!'

Ralph picked up the telephone and phoned the local planning authority straight away, but his worst fears were confirmed. Hanging up the phone he said, 'It's true. They have given permission for a developer to build 250 houses. The government has told them that we need to build millions more homes over the next decade.'

'Why do we need more houses?' asked Izzy, upset at the thought of the beautiful meadow being built on.

'Well, actually there are lots of reasons,' said Max, very reasonably. 'The way people live is changing. For example, people are living much longer, and young people are leaving home at a younger age, and they all need places to live. Also, more marriages are ending in divorce,' he added. 'And some people just prefer to live alone.'

'I suppose we do live in a beautiful place,' said Izzy, 'There are lots of jobs too. You can't blame people for wanting to move here from other parts of the country.'

'You can't blame them,' said Ralph, fuming, 'but I wish they would build the houses somewhere else!'

True or false?

The statements below give reasons why we need to build more houses. However, only some are true. Colour in all the labels that contain true statements.

- People are leaving home at a younger age.

- The population is falling.

- There is too much countryside.

- People are living longer.

- House prices are falling.

- People are getting married at an older age.

- More marriages are ending in divorce.

- People are migrating to other parts of the country.

- People don't like to live alone.

- Houses are getting bigger.

• TOP TIPS •

- The government expects 40% of new housing to be built on land that has not been built on before. This is known as greenfield land.

- Their target is that 60% of new housing will be built on brownfield land. These are areas in towns and cities which have been built on previously, and are now wasteland.

DID YOU KNOW?

1 England needs 4.4 million new homes between 2000 and 2016. This will result in the loss of countryside equivalent to 169 000 professional-sized football pitches.

2 At the same time it is estimated that there are 250 000 houses that currently have no one living in them!

Who would live in a place like this?

Izzy and Spotless were watching the archaeologists digging a trench through the meadow next to their house. (Spotless was hoping they might find some bones.) Max had explained that before the developers were allowed to build the new estate, an archaeological investigation had to take place, so that the history of the site could be recorded.

Izzy noticed that there appeared to be some excitement in the field. One of the archaeologists had found something. Izzy's curiosity got the better of her, and she leaped over the fence and walked towards the group of people.

'What have you found?' she asked.

'It's a Saxon brooch,' replied one of the archaeologists, holding up a gold-coloured piece of jewellery.

'Wow,' said Izzy. 'Were the Saxons the first people to live around here?'

'Well ... no. There is evidence of people first settling in this area over 6000 years ago,' replied the archaeologist, 'but it was the Saxons who really developed Oxford as a centre for trade.'

'Why do you think people wanted to live here?' asked Izzy.

'Well, this area had lots of things that people needed,' replied the archaeologist. 'The most important thing was the River Thames. The river provided a water supply, and also a transport route to London. Oxford was built at a point where it was possible to cross the river. That's where its name comes from: Oxen (another name for cattle) Ford (shallow crossing place in a river).'

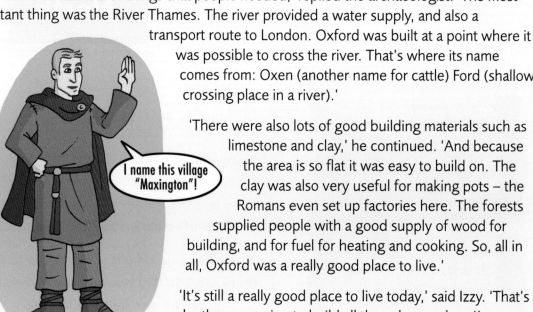

I name this village "Maxington"!

'There were also lots of good building materials such as limestone and clay,' he continued. 'And because the area is so flat it was easy to build on. The clay was also very useful for making pots – the Romans even set up factories here. The forests supplied people with a good supply of wood for building, and for fuel for heating and cooking. So, all in all, Oxford was a really good place to live.'

'It's still a really good place to live today,' said Izzy. 'That's why they are going to build all those houses here!'

Real or fake?

There are many strangely named places in the British Isles. Look carefully at the place names below, and try to decide whether you think they are real or fake by joining them to the correct signpost.

Belchertown

Ugley

Barton in the Beans

Nasty

Brown Willy

REAL

FAKE

Deadhorse

Little Boring

Little Snoring

Top Wallop

World's End

DID YOU KNOW?

Our ancestors were hunters and gatherers. They wandered from place to place hunting wild animals and collecting vegetables and berries. About 10 000 years ago, in the Middle East, people came up with the idea of farming, which meant they could now live in one place all the time. This was the beginning of settlement.

• TOP TIPS •

You can tell a lot about the history of a place from its name.

burg → fortified dwelling
by → homestead
thorpe → a new village
thwaite → meadow
ton → farming village

Everybody's going through changes

I'm going shopping. I've got absolutely nothing to wear!' announced Izzy

Max tried not to laugh, knowing that Izzy's wardrobe was full to bursting. 'How are you getting to the shops?' he asked.

'Oh, I thought I'd take the bus – it's better for the <u>environment</u> than being driven there in your car. See you later,' replied Izzy, as she closed the door behind her.

Izzy watched the passing scenery through the bus window. She noticed that the type of buildings changed along the way:

| On the edge of the city, where she lived, the houses were mainly <u>detached</u> and had large gardens. | → | Next came an area where the houses were <u>semi-detached</u>. | → | Then there were roads with <u>terraced</u> houses. | → | At one point she passed an old-fashioned looking factory with big iron gates next to the canal. | → | Finally, she reached the city centre with its large collection of shops. |

Later that day, when Izzy had returned home, she asked her dad about the changes she had noticed along the bus route.

'Mmmm,' Ralph replied. 'The <u>Central Business District</u>, with shops and offices, is always in the centre of a city, so that people can reach it easily from any direction.'

'That makes sense,' said Izzy, 'but what about the factory?'

Ralph continued, 'Well, back in the 1800s, there used to be factories around the city centre as well, and the terraced houses were often built close to the factories so the workers would have somewhere to live. Of course, most of the factories have now been knocked down, or converted. I expect the iron factory will be turned into apartments soon.'

I think I'd quite like to live in the CBD!

'That's sad,' said Izzy. 'Why do the houses get bigger away from the centre?'

'Well, the land gets cheaper the further you are away from the centre,' said Ralph, 'so people can afford to build bigger houses for the same amount of money.'

'So that also means that the oldest houses are in the centre, and the newest ones are on the outskirts,' suggested Izzy.

'That's right,' replied Ralph. 'Now, enough about houses – just how many new clothes did you buy?'

In the zone

Below is a simple model of the land use of a city.

Look at the pictures of different types of buildings. Now use a pencil to draw an arrow from each picture to the correct zone of the city.

DID YOU KNOW?

A mega-city is a settlement with a population of over 10 million people. The world's biggest mega-cities are listed below.

City	Population in 2000
Tokyo, Japan	28 025 000
Mexico City, Mexico	18 131 000
Mumbai, India	18 042 000
Sao Paulo, Brazil	17 711 000
New York City, USA	16 626 000
Shanghai, China	14 173 000
Lagos, Nigeria	13 488 000
Los Angeles, USA	13 129 000
Calcutta, India	12 900 000
Buenos Aires, Argentina	12 431 000

· TOP TIPS ·

Land use models are diagrams that explain how our towns and cities develop. The first land use model (the one on this page, above) was invented by an American man called Ernest Burgess in 1925 and – believe it or not – it is still used in Geography lessons today!

Test your knowledge 4

1 Answer the following questions

a) What is meant by the term 'greenfield land'?

....

b) What is meant by the term 'brownfield land'?

....

c) How many new houses are needed in England by 2016?

....

d) What percentage of these new houses should be built on brownfield land?

....

e) When did people first give up their nomadic lifestyles and begin living in settlements?

....

f) What is a mega-city?

....

(6 marks)

2 The sentences below give reasons why we need to build more houses in the UK. Complete them by filling in the missing words. You can use the words below.

> divorcing   married   migrating   increasing   living   leaving

a) People are .... home at a younger age.

b) The population is ....

c) People are .... longer.

d) People are getting .... at an older age.

e) People are .... more frequently.

f) People are .... to other parts of the country.

(6 marks)

34

3 Match the ancient settlement words with their meaning.

burg
by
thorpe
thwaite
ton

meadow
fortified dwelling
homestead
farming village
a new village

(5 marks)

4 Label the diagram to show why it is a good site for a settlement.

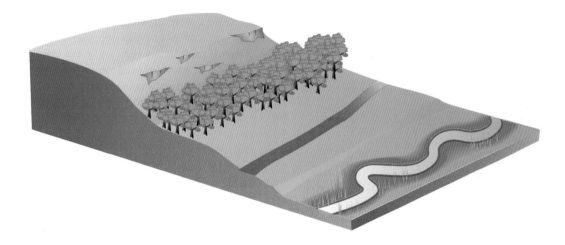

(8 marks)

5 Match the definitions with the correct key words.

Mixture of shops, offices and leisure facilities
Attached to other houses on both sides
Attached to another house on one side
Not attached to any other houses

Detached houses
Terraced houses
Central Business District (CBD)
Semi-detached houses

(4 marks)

(Total 29 marks)

How others see us

Izzy thundered down the stairs, a piece of paper flapping in her hand. 'Hey, slow down Izzy,' said Max. 'You'll wear out the carpet!'

'I'm sorry,' said Izzy. 'I'm just so excited. Abdul has sent me an email saying he and his family are coming to England on holiday, and they're arriving next week.'

'That's great,' said Ralph distractedly, as he poked at his latest invention (a clockwork toothbrush) with a screwdriver. 'Now, who is Abdul?'

'Oh, Dad, I've told you loads of times. He's my pen-pal in Bangladesh!' said Izzy.

'Oh, of course he is,' said Ralph. 'You will have to invite him and his family for dinner.'

Izzy sat down to read the email again more carefully.

'I'm going upstairs to email Abdul straight back,' said Izzy, folding her piece of paper in half. 'I need to tell him about the Queen, the weather and the mouldy cheese.'

'Really,' replied Max, 'I've not heard that one. You'll have to tell it to me later.'

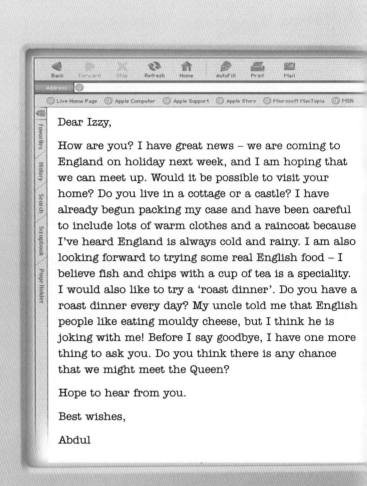

Dear Izzy,

How are you? I have great news – we are coming to England on holiday next week, and I am hoping that we can meet up. Would it be possible to visit your home? Do you live in a cottage or a castle? I have already begun packing my case and have been careful to include lots of warm clothes and a raincoat because I've heard England is always cold and rainy. I am also looking forward to trying some real English food – I believe fish and chips with a cup of tea is a speciality. I would also like to try a 'roast dinner'. Do you have a roast dinner every day? My uncle told me that English people like eating mouldy cheese, but I think he is joking with me! Before I say goodbye, I have one more thing to ask you. Do you think there is any chance that we might meet the Queen?

Hope to hear from you.

Best wishes,

Abdul

More tea Isabella?

It's not just cricket!

Guess which country these photos were taken in.

Country ....

· TOP TIPS ·

Our beliefs, opinions and ways of understanding things are known as <u>perception</u>. It is the 'way we see the world'. Often, people's perceptions can be inaccurate. Some people have an over-simplified and fixed impression about people, places and things. Such fixed impressions are known as <u>stereotypes</u>. For example, thinking that all French people like to eat snails and frogs' legs is a stereotype.

DID YOU KNOW?

Curry is the most popular takeaway food in England, closely followed by fish and chips, and then pizza.

Many 'Indian' restaurants in England are actually run by people of Bangladeshi descent.

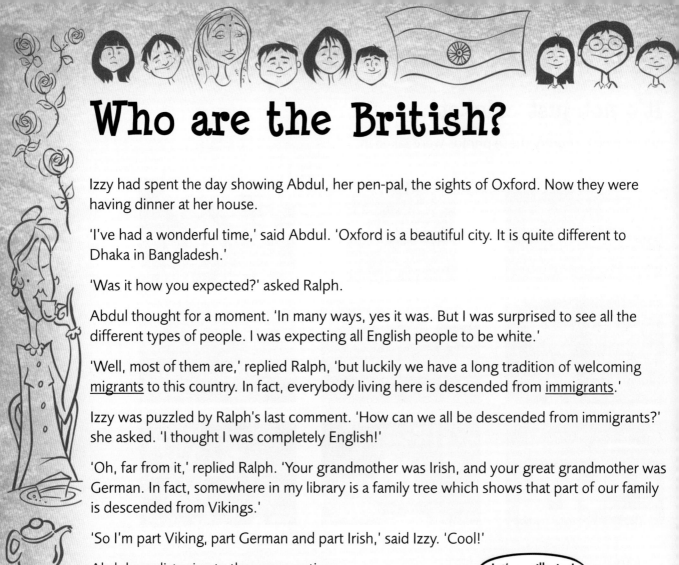

Who are the British?

Izzy had spent the day showing Abdul, her pen-pal, the sights of Oxford. Now they were having dinner at her house.

'I've had a wonderful time,' said Abdul. 'Oxford is a beautiful city. It is quite different to Dhaka in Bangladesh.'

'Was it how you expected?' asked Ralph.

Abdul thought for a moment. 'In many ways, yes it was. But I was surprised to see all the different types of people. I was expecting all English people to be white.'

'Well, most of them are,' replied Ralph, 'but luckily we have a long tradition of welcoming <u>migrants</u> to this country. In fact, everybody living here is descended from <u>immigrants</u>.'

Izzy was puzzled by Ralph's last comment. 'How can we all be descended from immigrants?' she asked. 'I thought I was completely English!'

'Oh, far from it,' replied Ralph. 'Your grandmother was Irish, and your great grandmother was German. In fact, somewhere in my library is a family tree which shows that part of our family is descended from Vikings.'

'So I'm part Viking, part German and part Irish,' said Izzy. 'Cool!'

Abdul was listening to the conversation carefully. 'So how much of Izzy is English?' he asked Ralph.

Let's go pillaging!

'Well, as I was saying,' replied Ralph, 'the English people are a mixture of a whole bunch of different races. The first people arrived from Europe about 6000 years ago, and they were followed by Celts, Romans, Saxons, Vikings, Normans and Huguenots.'

'Hugo-whats?' asked Izzy.

'Huguenots – people from France,' answered Ralph. 'More recently, people have come from further afield, places such as Jamaica, India, Pakistan, Bangladesh and China. It's part of what makes England such an interesting place to live.'

'It's certainly an interesting place to visit,' added Abdul, 'and you have all made me very welcome.'

Where are all the people from?

Using the list of original nationalities below, find the immigrants' countries of origin in the wordsearch.

K	U	Y	A	W	R	O	N	B	B
P	G	N	Y	L	A	T	I	A	L
F	A	C	N	G	P	S	Q	N	I
R	N	H	A	Z	A	J	C	G	W
A	D	I	M	T	K	Z	S	L	B
N	A	N	R	R	I	L	A	A	Q
C	O	A	E	X	S	R	J	D	R
E	W	Y	G	G	T	G	X	E	Y
T	I	R	E	L	A	N	D	S	C
I	N	D	I	A	N	W	Y	H	V

Italian
German
Norwegian
French
Irish
Indian
Pakistani
Bangladeshi
Chinese
Ugandan

DID YOU KNOW?

An immigrant is a person who moves to another country permanently. Thousands of years ago, no one lived here at all – so everyone in the United Kingdom is descended from immigrants. Some of the key immigrations are shown in the table below. Do you know who you are descended from?

Who?	Date
Romans	43
Saxons	500
Vikings	800
Normans	1066
Irish	1840
Italians	1946
West Indians	1948
Indians	1956
Pakistanis	1956
Bangladeshis	1971
Kosovans	1999

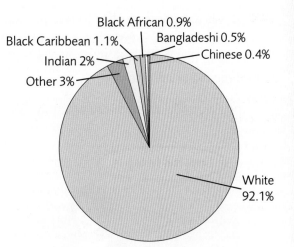

Black African 0.9%
Black Caribbean 1.1%
Bangladeshi 0.5%
Chinese 0.4%
Indian 2%
Other 3%
White 92.1%

• TOP TIPS •

The pie chart above shows the ethnic make up of the United Kingdom.

Wherever you lay your hat...

Izzy was studying her family tree. It was fascinating! She had not realised how interesting her ancestors were.

'Look, Max,' she said. 'It says here that Theobold Witherbottom emigrated to Brazil in search of Inca treasure in 1831, but he disappeared in the jungle and was never seen again. And here it shows that Tom Witherbottom emigrated to Japan in 1808 and became a legendary samurai warrior. But my favourite is this one – Katherine Witherbottom survived the sinking of the Titanic in 1912 on her way to begin a new life in the USA.'

'Well,' replied Max, 'travelling was certainly more dangerous back then, but your family obviously has an adventurous streak.'

'I think I do,' said Izzy. 'But what about you, Max, would you like to emigrate?'

'Well, I don't think I'd like to leave England for ever,' replied Max, 'but I did work in California as a butler to a famous singer a few years ago.'

'Wow!' exclaimed Izzy. 'How come?'

'Well, it was too good an offer to refuse,' replied Max. 'It was really good money and the lifestyle was fantastic – fast cars, a beautiful house in Beverly Hills, swimming in the morning and skiing in the afternoon. It was the middle of winter in England, so the wind and the rain helped me make my decision.'

'It sounds wonderful,' said Izzy wistfully. 'What on earth made you come back?'

I hope they let dogs in.

'Good question,' said Max. 'The singer got married to an English film producer and she came to live over here. I came as well, but to be honest she had become really moody and difficult to work for. When I saw your father's advert for a butler, I jumped at the chance of moving to Oxford and haven't looked back since.'

'Well, I'm glad you did,' said Izzy. 'I don't know where we'd be without you.'

Migration puzzle

Help the migrants below to find their new homes. Join each person to their new country with a line.

a)

b)

c)

Kenya France Spain Thailand Brazil Mexico

d)

e)

f)

DID YOU KNOW?

Migration is the movement of people within a country or between countries.

Migration can be permanent or temporary.

The reasons people migrate can be divided into 'push' factors and 'pull' factors.

Push factors are things that encourage people to leave, such as low standards of living or wars.

Pull factors are things that attract people to an area, such as a well-paid job and political freedom.

• TOP TIPS •

• Each year, about 500 000 people come to live in the UK.

• Each year, about 350 000 people leave the UK to live elsewhere.

• This means there is a net immigration of about 150 000 people a year.

Test your knowledge 5

1 Answer the questions below.

a) What is meant by the word 'perception'?

....

b) What is meant by the word 'stereotype'?

....

c) What is meant by the word 'migration'?

....

d) What is meant by the word 'immigrant'?

....

e) What percentage of the UK population is white?

....

f) How many migrants arrive in the UK each year?

....

g) How many people leave the UK each year?

....

(7 marks)

2 Join the pictures of food to the country you think they match best.

USA

China

France

Germany

England

Italy

Japan

Mexico

(8 marks)

3 Arrange the following list of immigrants to the British Isles in the order that they arrived.

Indians ....

Normans ....

Saxons ....

Bangladeshis ....

Vikings ....

Pakistanis ....

West Indians ....

Romans ....

(8 marks)

4 Divide the following into migration 'push factors' and 'pull factors'.

| Natural disasters | Good hospitals | Wars | Well-paid jobs |
| Good weather | Drought | Unemployment | Free education |

Push factors	Pull factors

(8 marks)

(Total 31 marks)

Six billion and counting

Izzy had just returned home after visiting her neighbour's new baby. Izzy wasn't really into babies – too much crying, sick and poo in her opinion.

Visiting the baby had made Izzy start to think. 'I wonder when the first human baby was born?' Never one to leave a question hanging in mid-air, she went looking for an answer. She began her search at the Pitt-Rivers museum in Oxford. She soon realised that this question was not an easy one to answer. She discovered the theory that our earliest ancestors were ape-like creatures that learned to walk upright about 4 million years ago. However, it was not until 100 000 years ago that 'homo sapiens' (people looking more or less like us) evolved in East Africa.

Gradually, human beings spread out from Africa to Europe, across to Asia, down to Australia, into North America and finally into South America. Of course, along the way people fell in love, got married, and more people were born. Despite this, the population grew very slowly because life was very dangerous. Many humans were eaten by predators such as sabre-toothed tigers, or died from diseases because there were no such things as hospitals.

Izzy looked at the next display board. It had the title 'Population explosion'. It showed that 2000 years ago there were only about 300 million people on the planet, but by 1800 this figure had reached 1 billion. It took 123 years for the population to double from 1 billion to 2 billion. However, it only took 12 years for the population to increase from 5 billion to 6 billion. The message was clear:

The world is filling up with humans... and fast!

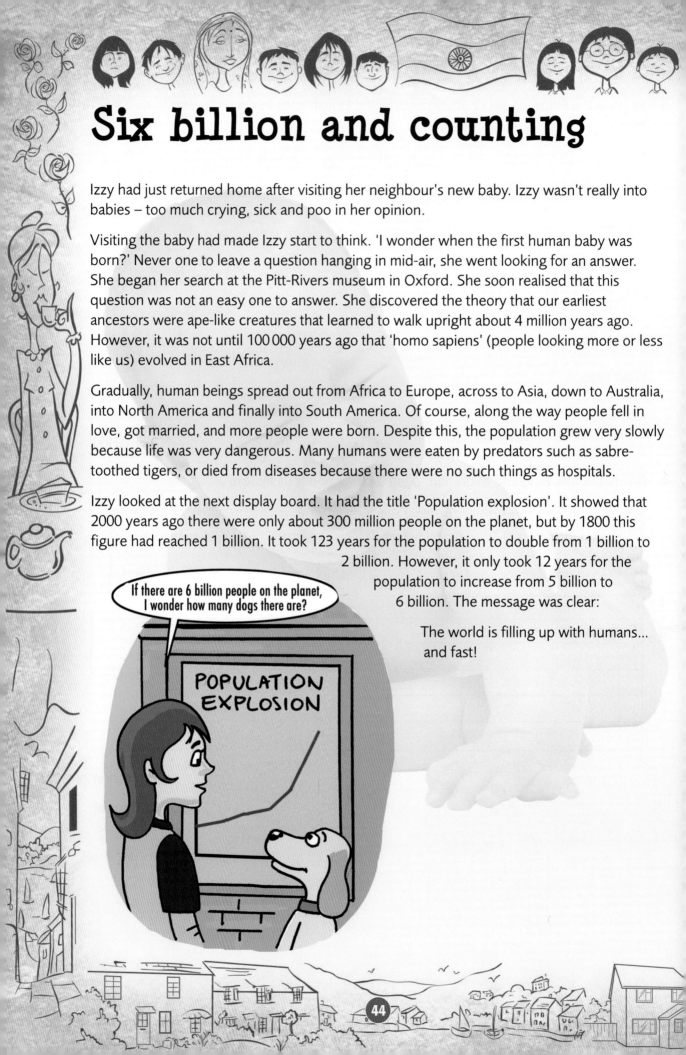

If there are 6 billion people on the planet, I wonder how many dogs there are?

POPULATION EXPLOSION

Counting pennies

The world's population has increased from 1 billion 200 years ago to 6.5 billion people today. Complete the puzzle to explain how this happened.

Imagine that on Day 1 you have one penny. On Day 2 it is doubled and you have two pence. On Day 3 it is doubled again and you have four pence, and so on. How many pennies, or pounds, would you have after 32 days?

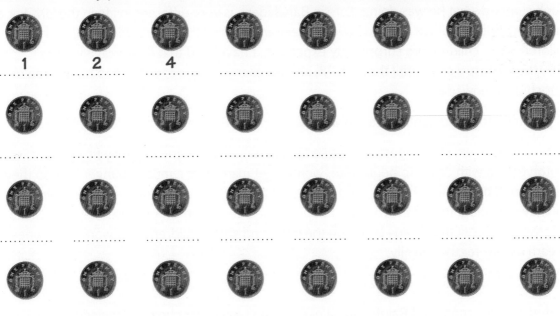

1 .... 2 .... 4 ....

....

....

....

The increase in the number of pennies represents what happens if the women of the world give birth to an average of four children each. In parts of the world, the average number is five!

· TOP TIPS ·

The rapid growth in global population since 1800 is known as the <u>population explosion</u>. It was caused by improvements in standards of living which reduced <u>death rates</u> while <u>birth rates</u> remained stable. Globally, birth rates are now falling and eventually the birth and death rates should be about the same.

DID YOU KNOW?

The world's population is thought to have reached 6 billion people in 1999. This number is continuing to grow at approximately 74 million people a year. The United Nations predicts that the global population growth is slowing down and that the figure will peak at 10.4 billion in 2200.

Where are all the babies?

'I'm bored,' said Izzy to Ralph, who was working on his latest invention (a self-cooling fizzy drink can). 'I wish I had a brother or sister to do things with. Abdul told me that in Bangladesh most families have at least three or four children. That would be really fun.'

Ralph stopped what he was doing. 'Life in Bangladesh is very different to life in the UK. For a start, most British women want to have a career and wait till they are older until they have children. Also, children are surprisingly expensive. I have read that on average it costs £100 000 to raise a child until they are 18, and not many people can afford to have three or four children nowadays.'

Izzy thought for a moment. 'I see. So why do people in Bangladesh have lots of children?'

'Mmm, another excellent question,' replied Ralph, who had begun carefully filling his prototype can with cola. 'To begin with, women get married at a much younger age, so they have more time to have children. And in some parts of the countryside, the more children you have the more important you are. People want lots of children because they are able to help with the work that needs doing on the farm, and some children even work in factories to earn money for their family.'

'I don't fancy doing that!' said Izzy.

'Unfortunately,' continued Ralph, 'many people don't have any choice. Bangladesh is a very poor country and many children die before they have a chance to grow up. That's another reason why it's important to have several children, especially since they are expected to look after their parents when they become old.'

'Do you want me to look after you when you are old?' asked Izzy.

'Well, I hope it won't be necessary,' replied Ralph, as the self-cooling can exploded, showering him and Izzy in cola froth, 'but thank you for asking.'

I have seven brothers and sisters. We don't get together very often now though!

Population clock

On average, four babies are born every second.

Fill in the gaps on the global population clocks below to work out how many babies are born each year.

Time	Number of babies
1 second	4
1 minute	☐ ☐ ☐
1 hour	☐ ☐ ☐ ☐ ☐
1 day	☐ ☐ ☐ ☐ ☐ ☐
1 month (31 days)	☐ ☐ ☐ ☐ ☐ ☐ ☐ ☐
1 year	☐ ☐ ☐ ☐ ☐ ☐ ☐ ☐ ☐

A bigger challenge! On average 107 people die every minute. Can you work out how many people die every year? ....

• TOP TIPS •

Today, people can use <u>birth control</u> methods to limit the size of their families, although not everybody has access to them or wants to use them. China takes birth control very seriously and has introduced strict rules which limit the number of babies. People who live in cities are limited to one child, while people who live in the countryside are allowed a second child if the first is a girl. Couples have to ask permission from the government before they are allowed to try for a baby!

DID YOU KNOW?

The number of people in the world increases by about 150 every minute, but this growth is not spread equally between countries. Out of every 100 babies born, 95 of them are born in poorer countries. This means that the populations of many poorer countries are rising rapidly, while in richer countries the population is actually falling.

An uneven world

'I've been thinking,' Ralph said. 'We've all been working very hard lately and could do with a holiday. I'd like to go somewhere really quiet where we can relax. We could take the tent!'

'That's fantastic, Dad,' replied Izzy, not terribly enthusiastically. 'But can't we go somewhere a bit more lively? You know, somewhere with hotels and shops and things to do?'

Ralph thought for a moment. 'I'll tell you what,' he said. 'Let's have a look in the atlas and try to decide together.'

Izzy and Ralph flicked through the pages of the atlas, stopping at a map of the world which showed the global <u>population distribution</u>.

'How about somewhere in Europe, like France or Germany?' asked Izzy, hopefully. 'Or what about the east coast of the USA? I bet New York is awesome!'

'I'm sure it is,' said Ralph, 'but how about visiting the Rockies in Canada, or even a trip up the Amazon in Brazil? I bet we wouldn't bump into many people there!'

'Exactly! That's why we should go somewhere like Japan with loads of interesting people to meet,' said Izzy. 'Or what about China? I saw a picture of Shanghai the other day. It looks really space age.'

I know that you wanted to get away from it all, Dad, but this is ridiculous!

'China would be fascinating, but there's over a billion people there already,' replied Ralph. 'How about a camel trek across the Sahara?'

Izzy laughed. 'Sand, sweat, stroppy camels and no showers – I don't think so!' she replied.

'Uh-hum,' coughed Max quietly from the doorway. 'I couldn't help overhearing your conversation, and I wondered whether you would like me to book the B&B on the Isle of Wight again this year?'

Izzy and Ralph looked at each other, and burst out laughing.

The perfect holiday

Help the two tourists to find their perfect holiday destinations.
Link them with arrows to the most suitable places.

I like to get away from it all, and visit places with hardly any people.

I like to visit places that are really busy, with lots of things to see and do.

• TOP TIPS •

The population of the world is spread out very unevenly. Most people live on only one third of the world's land surface. The most crowded areas are in Western Europe, India and China. The emptiest areas are in Canada, Brazil, north Africa, Russia and Australia.

Positive factors encourage people to live in an area:

- **Land which is flat or gently sloping.**
- **A climate with no extremes – warm with enough rain.**
- **Areas with plenty of resources, such as coal, minerals and timber.**
- **Areas with good access, such as the coast.**

Negative factors discourage people from living in an area:

- **Land which is mountainous and has steep slopes.**
- **An extreme climate – very hot, very cold and too dry.**
- **Areas with few natural resources.**
- **Areas with poor access, such as the middle of continents.**

Test your knowledge 6

1 Answer the following questions.

a) What is meant by the term 'population explosion'?

....

b) What caused the population explosion?

....

c) What has China done to limit its population growth?

....

d) Which is the world's most crowded country?

....

e) What is the approximate population of the world today?

....

(5 marks)

2 Fill in the gaps in the paragraph below. Use the words in the boxes.

Our earliest ancestors were ape-like creatures that lived about .... million
years ago. It was not until .... hundred thousand years ago that
'homo sapiens' evolved in East Africa. Gradually, human beings spread out from
Africa to ...., across to Asia, down to ...., into North
.... and finally into South America. .... thousand years ago
there were only about .... hundred million people on the planet, but by
1800 the population reached one .... This number doubled to two
billion by 1923, and reached .... billion in 1999. It is predicted that the
global population will peak at over .... billion in 2200.

| one | two | three | four | six | ten | billion |

| America | Europe | Australia |

(10 marks)

3 These statements are all about why people in poor countries have large families. Draw lines to show which are true and which are false.

a) Women get married at an old age.

b) Women with large families are respected.

c) Children are needed to work.

d) Infant death rates are low.

e) Children are expected to look after their parents when they are old.

f) Contraception is always available.

False   True

(6 marks)

4 Try to work out the population puzzle below.

240 babies are born into the world every minute. 107 people die every minute. By how many does the world's population increase each day? (There is room to note down your working.)

Global population increase per day: ....

(8 marks)

5 Classify the following statements into positive settlement factors or negative settlement factors.

Factor	Positive or negative?
a) Areas with good access, such as the coast	
b) Land which is flat or gently sloping	
c) Few natural resources	
d) A climate with no extremes – warm with enough rain	
e) Plenty of resources, such as coal, minerals and timber	
f) Areas with poor access, such as the middle of continents	
g) Land which is mountainous and has steep slopes	
h) An extreme climate – very hot, very cold or very dry	

(8 marks)

(Total 37 marks)

Flood alert

Max drew open the curtains in the living room, expecting to see the usual view of fields and houses, but something was very different. It took him a moment to realise what had happened.

'Ralph! Izzy! Wake up!' he called up the stairs. 'The river has <u>flooded</u>.'

Within minutes, Ralph and Izzy were staring out of the window at the new housing estate, which now appeared to have canals instead of roads.

'Wow!' said Izzy. 'The river must have burst its banks during the night.'

'Now then,' said Max urgently, 'the river might still be rising. We need to prepare in case it reaches us.'

So Max and Izzy spent the morning moving things upstairs. The sofas were too difficult to carry, so they decided to stack them on top of the dining room table.

'We must remember to turn off the electricity if the water gets too close,' said Max.

Meanwhile, Ralph filled up sandbags and placed them around the front door and back door. He hoped it would keep out the water if it did reach the house.

Finally, Ralph decided that it was now time to go and investigate. He managed to find an inflatable dinghy in the garage (they had bought it on holiday in Bognor Regis), and with Izzy set off towards the flood. Soon they were paddling through the streets of the housing estate. The water had risen to about three feet and people were leaving, or being evacuated, from their homes.

'Our house is ruined,' shouted one lady who was being carried out by a fireman. 'We've lost the carpets, the sofas, the TV, the DVD player, the fridge, and the cat's gone missing.'

'It's terrible,' said Izzy. 'Look, even the cars are full of water!'

'You're right,' said Ralph. 'But the worst thing isn't the water, it's all the mud and sewage it brings with it. Come on we'd better get back to our house.'

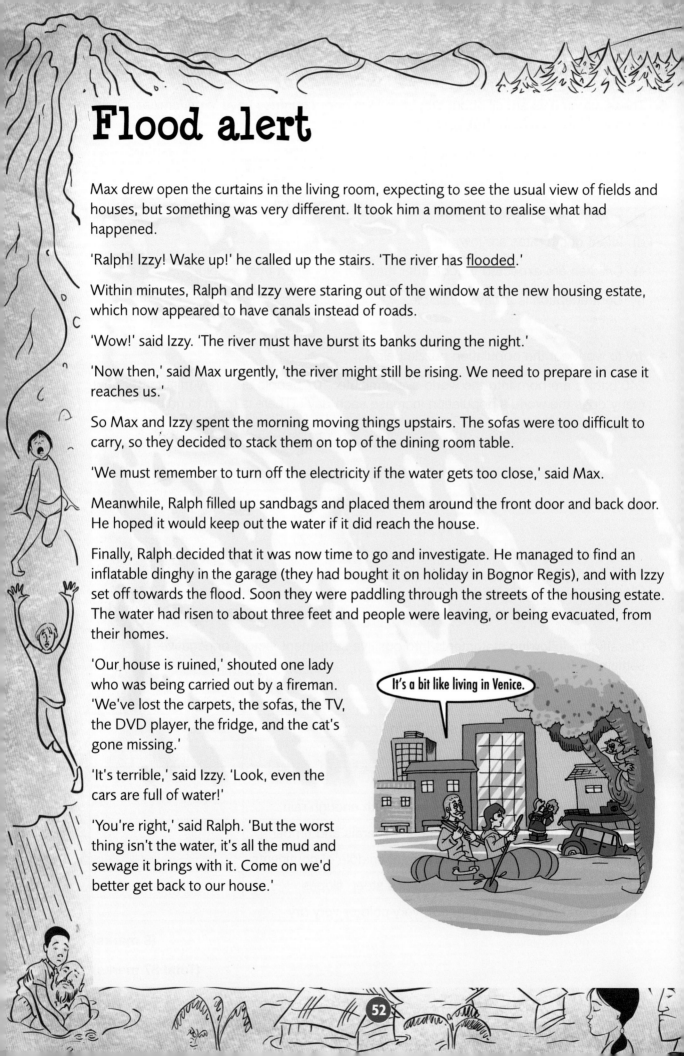

It's a bit like living in Venice.

Odd ones out

Help to protect the house before the flood arrives. Draw a circle around the sandbags that contain the effects of flooding. Be careful, some of them are red herrings!

Carpets ruined

Heavy rainfall

People evacuated

Thunder-storm

Cars damaged

River burst banks

Transport difficult

Snow melting

Sewage contamin-ation

Power cuts

· TOP TIPS ·

Find out if your house is at risk from flooding by using the interactive flood map on the Environment Agency's website. The site also contains lots of information about what to do in the event of a flood.

DID YOU KNOW?

Floods are the world's most dangerous natural disaster. On average, they kill more people each year than any other natural hazard, including earthquakes and volcanic eruptions.

After the flood

The floodwaters had subsided without reaching 24 Blenheim Gardens. However, the clean-up operation continued over at the housing estate, and elsewhere in the city. Over 400 houses had been flooded, and millions of pounds worth of damage had been done. It would be months before the houses dried out and life could return to normal. The flood had worried Izzy, and she set about trying to find out why such an awful thing had happened.

She learned from a TV report on the local news that a <u>warm front</u> and a <u>cold front</u> had collided, causing especially heavy rain. The rain had been unable to sink into the ground quickly enough because the rock in the surrounding area – mainly clay – is <u>impermeable</u>. Instead, the water had run across the land into the River Thames and headed towards Oxford, where it met the Oxford Canal. The rivers had not been able to hold all the water and so they had burst their banks flooding the area around them.

Izzy found Max, who was emptying out sandbags in the garden. She explained the cause of the flood to him.

'I'm sure that's true, Izzy,' he said. 'But, you know, rivers are supposed to flood. That's what they have been doing for millions of years – flooding and depositing silt on the <u>floodplain</u>. The problem is that people keep building houses on the floodplain, and then they are surprised when the river comes through their front door.'

'Every time we cut down more trees,' Max continued, 'and build more houses, less rainfall is soaked up, so more water ends up in the rivers, and the more floods we have!' He tipped out the last sandbag.

'I see,' said Izzy. 'So the rain causes floods, but people can make them worse.'
'Exactly,' said Max.

Well, Spotless, the ark is nearly finished. We've got one dog- we just need all the other animals now.

Flood crossword

Complete the crossword about flooding using the clues.

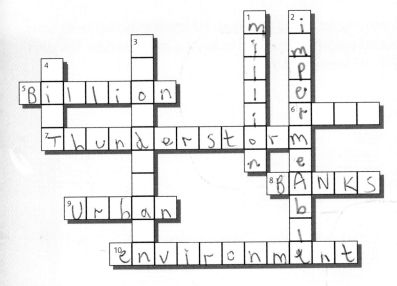

Crossword solution grid:
- 1 down: million
- 2 down: impermeable
- 3 down: floodplain
- 4 down: silt
- 5 across: Billion
- 6 across: rain
- 7 across: Thunderstorm
- 8 across: BANKS
- 9 across: Urban
- 10 across: environment

Across

5. Flooding causes one ...... pounds worth of damage a year in England and Wales.
6. Warm fronts and cold fronts bring ......
7. A flash flood is caused by a ......
8. A river floods when it bursts its ......
9. Flash floods are most common in ...... areas and deserts.
10. The ...... Agency is responsible for giving flood warnings.

Down

1. Five ...... people live in flood risk areas in England and Wales.
2. Clay is an ...... rock.
3. A ...... is an area of flat land next to a river.
4. Rivers deposit ...... on the floodplain.

DID YOU KNOW?

Around 5 million people, in 2 million houses, live in areas at risk from flooding in England and Wales. Each year flooding in these two countries causes about £1 billion worth of damage. The Environment Agency is responsible for warning people about floods, and trying to prevent them. You can call them on 0845 988 1188 to find out if a river near you is likely to flood.

• TOP TIPS •

A flash flood is a sudden and severe flood that can cause a huge amount of damage very quickly. Flash floods happen after a burst of heavy rainfall during a thunderstorm. They are especially likely in urban areas where the ground is impermeable, or in areas such as deserts where the ground has been baked hard.

Holding back the water

Ralph had also been doing some thinking following the flood. He knew they had been lucky this time. But what if the river flooded again? He made it his mission over the next few days to learn as much as he could about preventing floods.

Flood prevention for rivers

The most effective method is to build a dam. However, these cost millions of pounds to build.

Dams need deep valleys to store the water in a reservoir - which is no good in a county as flat as Oxfordshire.

I think that the best solution is to plant more trees to absorb rainwater, and to stop building houses on floodplains.

A good solution is to make the river bigger so it holds more water. This can be done by widening it, or deepening it, or even by building large walls called embankments along the side of the river.

Another drastic solution is to straighten the river by cutting off the river meanders. This makes the water travel faster so there is less chance of it flooding.

Food prevention for the home

Look at the Environment Agency's website for advice on flood prevention in your home.

There are special guards to make doors and windows waterproof in minutes.

A huge rubber ring, pumped full of water, can go around the house and prevent water reaching the bricks.

You can buy a plastic 'skirt' to go around your house so water will not soak into the bricks.

Houses can even be built on stilts.

Scrambled words

Rearrange the scrambled words to identify a range of flood control methods.

1. APTLN TSREE   _ _ _ _ _ _ / _ _ _ _ _ _

2. VIORSERRE   _ _ _ _ _ _ _ _ _

3. NATMNKEEMB   _ _ _ _ _ _ _ _ _ _ _

4. DMA   _ _ _

5. ILAFNGOT SUSOEH   _ _ _ _ _ _ _ _ _ / _ _ _ _ _ _ _

6. IGOZNN   _ _ _ _ _ _ _

7. NNGEIWDI   _ _ _ _ _ _ _ _ _

8. GEEPDENIN   _ _ _ _ _ _ _ _ _ _

9. DROO ARDGU   _ _ _ _ / _ _ _ _ _

10. GNHGEIITRANTS   _ _ _ _ _ _ _ _ _ _ _ _

DID YOU KNOW?

Half of the Netherlands is below sea level, so the Dutch have to take flood control very seriously. They have held back the sea and built embankments alongside rivers for hundreds of years. Now they are looking at a new solution – houses on stilts and houses that float. One company has designed and built a range of houses next to a river that will rise and fall with the floodwaters. Visit www.h2olland.nl to see some pictures.

• TOP TIPS •

- Flood control methods such as dams and embankments are known as <u>hard engineering</u>. Hard engineering is very expensive to build and maintain.

- Methods such as planting trees and zoning (banning house-building in high risk areas) are known as <u>soft engineering</u>. Soft engineering is a more natural solution to flooding.

Test your knowledge 7

1 Answer the following questions.

a) What is the name of the organisation that is responsible for monitoring floods in England and Wales?

....

b) What is a 'flash flood'?

....

c) Where are flash floods most likely to occur?

....

d) How many houses in England and Wales are at risk from flooding?

....

e) What is the approximate cost of damage caused by flooding in England and Wales each year?

....

f) What is the difference between 'hard' and 'soft' flood control techniques?

....

(6 marks)

2 Some of the following are sensible things to do in the event of a river flood. Draw lines to show which are sensible and which are daft.

a) Put sticky tape around your doors and windows.

b) Move furniture upstairs.

c) Dig a moat around your house.

d) Turn off the electricity.

e) Pile sandbags in front of doors.

f) Take your canoe for a paddle.

g) Evacuate the area.

h) Take up carpets.

i) Go swimming.

j) Call the coastguard.

(5 marks)

3 Describe five effects of flooding in the UK.

a) ....

b) ....

c) ....

d) ....

e) ....

(5 marks)

4 Circle the following statements that are genuine causes of flooding.

a) A fall in sea level

b) A long period of rainfall

c) A thunderstorm during the summer

d) Planting forests

e) Impermeable rock such as clay

f) Snow melt in spring

g) Permeable rock such as chalk

h) Building on the flood plain

i) Cutting down trees

j) The river burst its banks

(5 marks)

5 Match the following flood control methods to the correct descriptions below.

a) A wall across a river which traps water in a reservoir	
b) The river bottom is dredged so it can hold more water	
c) Walls are built alongside the river so it can hold more water	
d) River meanders are cut-off so the river becomes shorter	
e) Prevent building in areas which are at risk of flooding	
f) Watertight barriers placed in front of doors and windows	

Zoning   Deepen   Straighten   Dam   Flood guards   Embankment

(6 marks)

(Total 27 marks)

Flood disaster in Bangladesh

Izzy had emailed Abdul to tell him about the flood in Oxford. She was expecting to hear back from him, but she was very shocked by his reply. Apparently it had flooded in Bangladesh as well, but the scale of the disaster was far beyond her imagining. Her excitement at receiving the email turned to sadness as she read.

Address: http://www.deliaonline.com/cookeryschool/howto/how_0000000012.asp

Live Home Page | Apple Computer | Apple Support | Apple Store | Microsoft MacTopia | MSN

Dear Izzy,

I am sorry to hear that it has flooded in Oxford. We know all about floods in Bangladesh as the rivers burst their banks every year, but this summer has been especially bad.

The River Brahmaputra and River Ganges have overflowed and submerged half of the country. In Dhaka, where I live, three quarters of the city is under two metres of water. It has been like this for two months now and the water level is only just beginning to go down.

The news reports tell us that across the whole of Bangladesh over 500 people have died and 25 million people have lost their homes – 25 million homeless! Farmers have lost half of their crops, and thousands of cows have been drowned, so in some places there are terrible food shortages. People have to live on biscuits and rice given to them by aid organisations like Oxfam. We also have many power cuts and some people have no electricity at all.

But, the biggest problem is drinking water. Dead animals and sewage have contaminated the wells and people are becoming ill with diarrhoea and typhoid. Luckily, we can afford to buy bottled water, but the situation is truly terrible for so many people. I do hope the flood will be over soon and life can begin to get back to normal.

With best regards,

Abdul

Izzy sat stunned for a while. She felt really sorry for the people of Bangladesh, and slightly guilty for telling Abdul how bad the Oxford floods had been. Unable to do anything practical to help, she decided that she would give this month's pocket money to Oxfam to help pay for emergency aid supplies.

Flooding wordsearch

Find the words to do with flooding listed in the wordsearch.

J	P	O	A	K	S	C	Z	C	K	E	O	F	F	B
H	H	S	T	J	Z	U	E	L	O	A	K	F	A	Z
G	A	L	T	U	H	W	B	B	H	B	J	N	B	I
X	I	R	V	U	C	N	D	M	I	A	G	C	K	F
S	E	A	T	W	C	V	K	A	E	L	W	G	B	S
F	E	N	T	U	W	R	E	D	A	R	E	T	S	E
D	G	P	W	I	P	O	E	D	U	D	G	Q	Q	B
R	G	Z	S	C	H	A	E	W	X	P	I	E	R	N
O	Y	A	E	R	O	S	M	M	O	F	X	Z	D	Z
W	Q	W	R	Y	H	D	N	H	R	P	C	S	O	Q
N	P	A	L	V	Y	H	E	X	A	M	X	F	U	Y
E	I	B	S	P	O	R	C	B	B	R	P	H	G	E
D	H	O	M	E	L	E	S	S	Z	O	B	Z	A	T
P	S	E	G	N	A	G	M	J	T	I	L	P	W	Q
T	Y	P	H	O	I	D	N	O	M	V	Z	A	U	S

Brahmaputra Ganges Submerged Homeless Drowned
Power cuts Diarrhoea Typhoid Bangladesh Crops

DID YOU KNOW?

Flooding is the world's most dangerous disaster, but most deaths are not caused by the floodwater itself.
• People die mainly from diseases such as diarrhoea and dysentery.
• Stagnant pools allow malaria-carrying mosquitoes to breed.
• People whose crops and animals have been lost may die from starvation unless they are lucky enough to receive emergency food aid.
• An unlucky few even die from snake bites when they climb up a tree to get above the floodwater, and find they are sharing their refuge with an angry cobra!

DID YOU KNOW?

Mosquito facts:
• Mosquitoes have been on the planet for 170 million years.
• An average mosquito weights 2 milligrams.
• Mosquitoes live for up to 100 days.
• Mosquitoes can even survive in the Arctic Circle, where they spend the winter frozen in ice.
• Mosquitoes transmit malaria, yellow fever, jungle fever and dengue fever.
• Mosquitoes can detect the heat of a human being from 3 metres away.
• Mosquitoes feed on plant nectar, but need blood to develop their eggs.
• There are between 350 million and 500 million cases of malaria globally every year.
• One million people die from malaria annually.

Why are there floods?

Izzy had been really shocked when she heard about the flooding in Bangladesh from Abdul. She went to talk to her father about it.

'Yes, I know Izzy,' said Ralph. 'It's terrible. There have been lots of reports about the floods in the newspapers.'

'Why does it flood so badly in Bangladesh?' she asked him.

Ralph put down his newspaper. 'Well, to begin with Bangladesh has over 250 rivers, and three really large ones: the Ganges, Brahmaputra and Meghna. Many of the rivers start in the foothills of the Himalayas, and are fed by water from melting ice in the summer. The problem is that Bangladesh also receives most of its monsoon rainfall during the summer. Most years the amount of water is just too much for the rivers to cope with.'

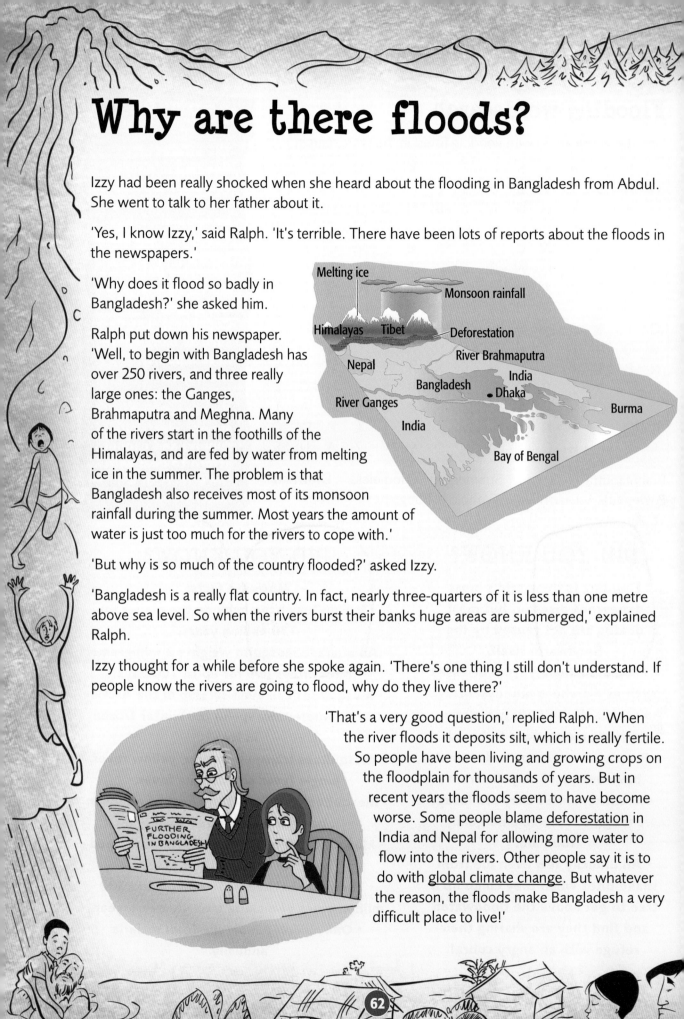

Map labels: Melting ice, Monsoon rainfall, Himalayas, Tibet, Deforestation, River Brahmaputra, Nepal, India, Bangladesh, Dhaka, River Ganges, India, Burma, Bay of Bengal

'But why is so much of the country flooded?' asked Izzy.

'Bangladesh is a really flat country. In fact, nearly three-quarters of it is less than one metre above sea level. So when the rivers burst their banks huge areas are submerged,' explained Ralph.

Izzy thought for a while before she spoke again. 'There's one thing I still don't understand. If people know the rivers are going to flood, why do they live there?'

'That's a very good question,' replied Ralph. 'When the river floods it deposits silt, which is really fertile. So people have been living and growing crops on the floodplain for thousands of years. But in recent years the floods seem to have become worse. Some people blame <u>deforestation</u> in India and Nepal for allowing more water to flow into the rivers. Other people say it is to do with <u>global climate change</u>. But whatever the reason, the floods make Bangladesh a very difficult place to live!'

Kriss kross

Complete the crossword about the causes of flooding in Bangladesh.

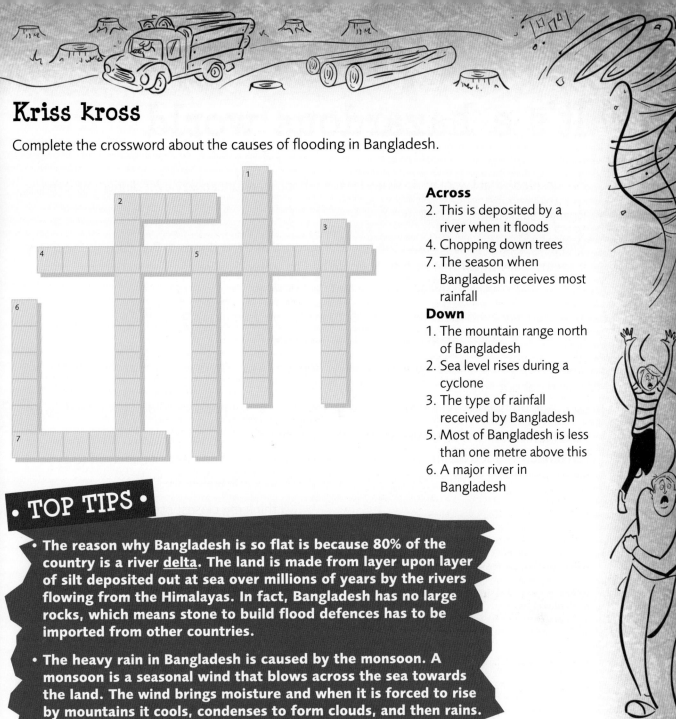

Across
2. This is deposited by a river when it floods
4. Chopping down trees
7. The season when Bangladesh receives most rainfall

Down
1. The mountain range north of Bangladesh
2. Sea level rises during a cyclone
3. The type of rainfall received by Bangladesh
5. Most of Bangladesh is less than one metre above this
6. A major river in Bangladesh

• TOP TIPS •

- The reason why Bangladesh is so flat is because 80% of the country is a river <u>delta</u>. The land is made from layer upon layer of silt deposited out at sea over millions of years by the rivers flowing from the Himalayas. In fact, Bangladesh has no large rocks, which means stone to build flood defences has to be imported from other countries.

- The heavy rain in Bangladesh is caused by the monsoon. A monsoon is a seasonal wind that blows across the sea towards the land. The wind brings moisture and when it is forced to rise by mountains it cools, condenses to form clouds, and then rains.

DID YOU KNOW?

Flooding in Bangladesh is made worse by tropical <u>cyclones</u>, the same thing as a hurricane. Torrential rain swells the rivers, but at the same time low air pressure causes the sea to rise by up to 5 metres (storm surge). The sea floods the coastal areas, and the rivers have nowhere to go, flooding the land on either side of them.

It's a hazardous world

'I've decided what I want to do when I leave school,' announced Izzy over dinner one evening.

'Really?' said Ralph. 'Do tell us.'

'Well, I've been thinking about the floods in Oxford and the floods in Bangladesh,' said Izzy. 'It seems really unfair that so many people had to suffer. So I've decided to become a river expert. That way I can design ways to control flooding.'

'That's a really good idea,' said Max. 'But perhaps you shouldn't specialise too soon.'
'How do you mean?' asked Izzy.

'Well, the world can be a dangerous place,' replied Max. 'There are plenty of natural hazards to worry about apart from flooding. Why, it seems like only yesterday that I was caught in a <u>hurricane</u> on holiday in Florida. I had to tie myself to a palm tree so I didn't get blown away!'

'And I remember the time I was driving through Oklahoma on the way to an inventor's convention,' added Ralph. 'Suddenly a <u>tornado</u> came out of nowhere. I managed to avoid it with some skilful driving, but the cows in the next field weren't so lucky.'

'I think *my* closest escape was when I was in Japan studying Karate,' said Max. 'There was a huge <u>earthquake</u> one morning, which caused a massive <u>landslide</u>, followed by a <u>tsunami</u> that hit the coast an hour later. My house was never the same again.'

'Wasn't it in Japan that you were buried by an <u>avalanche</u> when you were snowboarding off-piste?' prompted Ralph.

'No, that was in France,' replied Max. 'Luckily I was found by a very good sniffer dog. 'Woof, woof,' Spotless voiced his approval.

'And what about the time I had to escape the forest fire that had been started by an erupting <u>volcano</u> in Indonesia? For a while I...'

'OK, OK, I get it!' exclaimed Izzy. 'There are loads of different natural hazards in the world apart from flooding. I obviously need to have a re-think about my career.'

'Have you ever thought about becoming a geography teacher?' asked Ralph.

Izzy rolled her eyes upwards and decided the best thing was to concentrate on her spaghetti bolognese.

Hazard word ladder

Complete the word ladder using the clues below to reveal a hidden word.

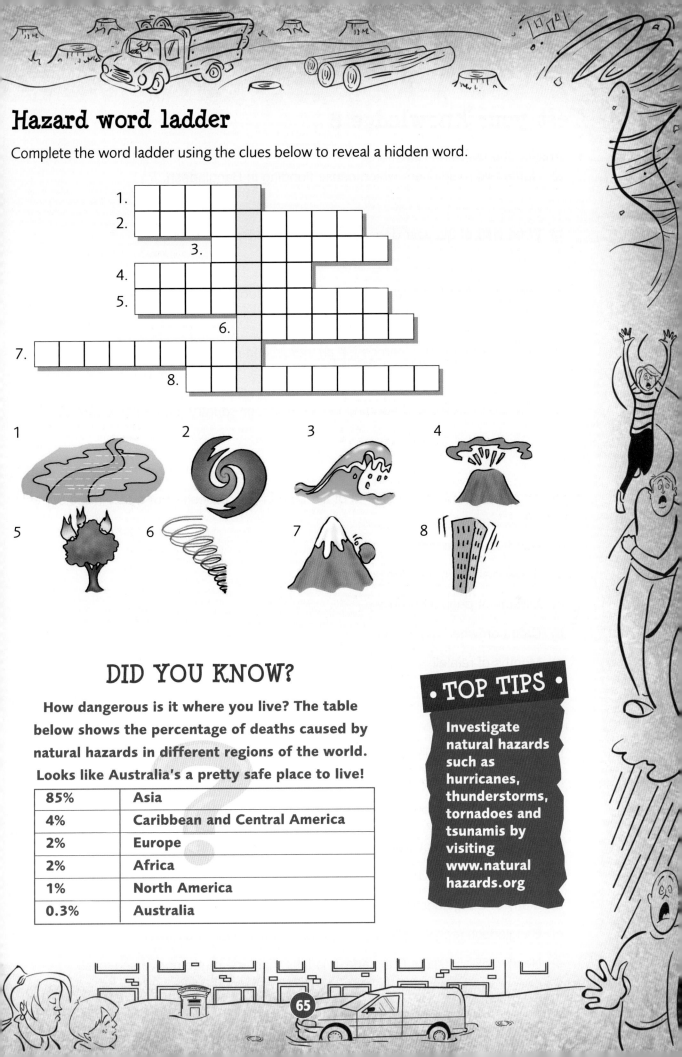

1.
2.
3.
4.
5.
6.
7.
8.

1   2   3   4

5   6   7   8

DID YOU KNOW?

How dangerous is it where you live? The table below shows the percentage of deaths caused by natural hazards in different regions of the world. Looks like Australia's a pretty safe place to live!

85%	Asia
4%	Caribbean and Central America
2%	Europe
2%	Africa
1%	North America
0.3%	Australia

· TOP TIPS ·

Investigate natural hazards such as hurricanes, thunderstorms, tornadoes and tsunamis by visiting www.natural hazards.org

Test your knowledge 8

1 Answer the following questions.

a) Name two main rivers which cause flooding in Bangladesh.

....

b) What time of the year does flooding occur in Bangladesh?

....

c) How does flooding in a poor country cause food shortages?

....

d) Explain how flooding can cause an increase in malaria.

....

e) Why are the effects of flooding worse in a poor country than a rich country?

....

(5 marks)

2 Which of the following are effects of flooding in Bangladesh? Put a tick in the correct boxes.

a) Hundreds of deaths ☐

b) Snow melting in the Himalayas ☐

c) Millions of people homeless ☐

d) Crops drowned and ruined ☐

e) Months of rainfall ☐

f) Thunderstorm ☐

g) Animals drowned ☐

h) Contaminated drinking water ☐

i) Snake bites ☐

j) Rivers burst their banks ☐

(6 marks)

3 Cross out the incorrect words in the sentences below.

a) Bangladesh has over *250 / 500* rivers.

b) Many of Bangladesh's rivers begin in the foothills of the *Alps / Himalayas*.

c) Bangladesh receives monsoon rainfall in the *summer / autumn*.

d) Nearly *75% / 50%* of Bangladesh is less than one metre above sea level.

e) When the river floods it deposits *infertile / fertile* silt on the floodplain.

f) Deforestation in *India / Thailand* may be contributing to flooding in Bangladesh.

g) Eighty percent of Bangladesh is a river *meander / delta*.

h) Tropical cyclones can cause the sea to rise by up to *five / twenty* metres.

(8 marks)

4 Match the natural hazards with their correct definition.

Volcano	Flood	Hurricane	Tsunami
Tornado	Earthquake	Landslide	Avalanche

Definition	Natural hazard
a) An overflow of a large amount of water on to an area that is usually dry	
b) A tropical storm with powerful winds and very heavy rainfall	
c) A powerful rotating column of air	
d) Shockwaves caused by sudden movements of rock beneath the Earth's surface	
e) A sudden movement of soil and rock down a slope	
f) A very large sea wave usually caused by an earthquake	
g) A mass of snow and ice sliding rapidly down a mountainside	
h) An opening in the Earth's crust which erupts ash, lava and gas	

(8 marks)

5 Arrange the following places in order of danger from natural hazards.

North America
Europe
Africa
Asia
Australia
Caribbean and Central America

Most dangerous
Least dangerous

(5 marks)

(Total 32 marks)

The Olympics

Since the announcement that the 2012 Olympic Games will be held in London, the Olympics had been a hot topic of conversation in Izzy's family.

Izzy, Ralph and Max were having dinner out in a Greek restaurant and reminiscing about when they went to see the 2004 Olympics in Athens, Greece.

Izzy wondered aloud, 'I wonder how they decide where to hold the Olympics?'

After swallowing his mouthful of moussaka, Ralph said, 'It's all a question of geography ... and a bit of politics as well.'

'How do you mean?' asked Izzy.

'Well, any country can apply to host the Olympics,' answered Ralph. 'However, the final decision is made by the International Olympic Committee based on a whole range of different factors. To begin with they need to be sure that the government, and public, are up for it. It takes years to organise and costs millions to build all the stadiums. Of course, it helps if they have good sports facilities already!'

Although the original Olympics date back to ancient Greece, the modern games were founded by a French man called Baron Pierre de Coubertin. The first modern games took place in Athens in 1896. Only 14 countries took part. Since then there have been 26 summer Olympics and 20 winter Olympics. The 2008 summer Olympics are to be held in Beijing, China, for the first time.

Sorry, Spotless, I don't think dogs are allowed to compete!

Max joined in, 'The IOC also need to be sure that the country's infrastructure is good enough. Things like roads, railways and airports are really important with so many people visiting the country. And nowadays they expect the host country to consider how the Olympics can improve the environment as well.'

'And don't forget about having enough hotels,' said Ralph. 'They don't want people having to sleep in bus shelters!'

There was a pause in the conversation.

'Like we did when we arrived in Athens, you mean?' asked Izzy.

'Yes ... well ... I thought Max had booked the hotel,' answered Ralph sheepishly. 'And anyway, it was a very clean bus shelter.'

Name the Olympic cities

The cities on the map have all hosted the Olympic games. How many can you name?

Unscramble these city names to help you.

A KOOTY _ _ _ _ _

B MXOEICCYTI _ _ _ _ _ _ / _ _ _ _

C MCHINU _ _ _ _ _ _

D MLROTANE _ _ _ _ _ _ _ _

E MOOCSW _ _ _ _ _ _

F LSOAEGLNES _ _ _ / _ _ _ _ _ _ _

G SLOUE _ _ _ _ _

H BAELROANC _ _ _ _ _ _ _ _ _

I AATANLT _ _ _ _ _ _ _

J SYDEYN _ _ _ _ _ _

K ANSTHE _ _ _ _ _ _

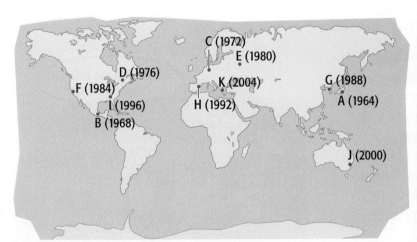

Baron Pierre de Couberton

TOP TIPS

- **Have you heard this saying before? It is the Olympic creed, attributed to Baron Pierre de Coubertin, the founder of the modern Olympic Games. Do you think this belief still holds true in sport today?**

  'The most important thing in the Olympic Games is not to win but to take part, just as the most important thing in life is not the triumph but the struggle. The essential thing is not to have conquered but to have fought well.'

DID YOU KNOW?

- The first recorded ancient Olympic Games took place in 776 BC in a place called Olympia – hence the name!

- The games were a sporting festival in honour of Zeus, the king of the Greek gods.

- Only Greeks were allowed to compete in the ancient Olympic Games but, like today, they were held every four years.

Olympic winners and losers

'I was wondering,' said Izzy, 'why do countries want to host the Olympics? It must be a lot of hassle!'

'You're right,' replied Ralph. 'It's a huge amount of work. But if things work out it can be really good for the country. Remember that over three billion people watch the Olympics on television. It raises the country's profile, and attracts lots of tourists.'

'And think about all the sponsorship,' said Max. 'Companies like Coca Cola and McDonalds pay a fortune to be allowed to put the Olympic symbol on their products. The Sydney Olympics in 2000 generated over one and a half billion pounds from ticket sales, TV rights and sponsorship deals.'

'Wow, that's amazing,' said Izzy. 'But surely it isn't all about money?'

'No, you are quite right,' said Max. 'There are lots of different reasons. One of the most important nowadays is using the Olympics to bring money to a run-down area to help regenerate it. In Sydney, they cleaned up an old polluted industrial wasteland for the site of the main stadium. That probably wouldn't have happened without the Olympics.'

'It's not all good news though,' chipped in Ralph. 'Sometimes a country spends too much money on the preparation and they end up in debt.'

'I was reading in the paper,' added Max, 'that the Athens games cost £4 billion pounds to host, and the Greek politicians are already arguing about what is going to happen to all the sports stadiums they built. They aren't all needed now the games are over, but they will cost millions to maintain.'

'Gosh, you don't think about all this when you see an athlete winning a gold medal,' said Izzy. 'Perhaps it would be simpler if the Olympics were always held in Greece, like in ancient times.'

'Now there's an idea!' said Ralph and Max in unison.

The top ten

Match the top ten gold medal-winning countries with the correct flags.

You will need to find out which countries the flags belong to first!

Germany   Great Britain   France   USA   Italy   Australia
China   Japan   Russia   South Korea

a)		[USA flag]
b)		[China flag]
c)		[flag]
d)		[Australia flag]
e)		[Japan flag]
f)		[Germany flag]
g)		[flag]
h)		[flag]
i)		[South Korea flag]
j)		[Great Britain flag]

• TOP TIPS •

The Olympic symbol of five interlocking rings represents the five <u>continents</u> of the Americas, Europe, Asia, Africa and Oceania. Seventy eight percent of the world's population recognises the symbol. That's more than recognise the Red Cross, and means that it is worth a lot of money in sponsorship deals!

DID YOU KNOW?

The Sydney Olympics in 2000 were billed as the first 'green' games. Solar-powered security vehicles patrolled the Olympic village, while solar panels were also fitted at some sports stadiums. Large areas of polluted wasteland were cleared up for stadiums and new housing.

'A journey of a thousand miles begins with a single step' (Chinese proverb)

Izzy had really enjoyed her visit to Athens to see the Olympic Games. In fact, she had enjoyed it so much that she managed to persuade her father that they should visit the next Games. This would be in Beijing, China, in 2008. Ralph had given Izzy the job of planning the journey, and she wasted no time in getting started. First she visited a travel agent in Oxford.

'Hello, I'd like to know how much a flight from London to Beijing costs please,' she said to the sales assistant.

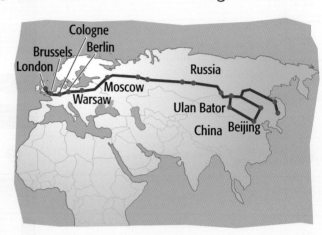

'Really? Beijing?' replied the lady. 'Are you sure you wouldn't rather go to Ibiza or Tenerife?'

But Izzy insisted that she was not into sunbathing, and eventually managed to find out that a return flight would cost about £500. Apparently a direct flight took about 10 hours, and Beijing was 8 hours ahead of British time, so if they left at midday they wouldn't arrive until 6 o'clock the next morning. Of course, on the way back, they would arrive only two hours after the time they left! Izzy found that thinking about this made her head hurt, and she suspected it would involve serious 'jet-lag'.

She explained all this to Max when she returned home. He suggested that she investigated something called the 'Trans-Siberian Railway' as an alternative.

I wonder if they have English takeaways in China?

Izzy looked it up on the Internet, and discovered that it was in fact possible to travel all the way from London to Beijing by train! The first part of the journey involved taking the Eurostar from London to Brussels, and from Brussels it was a two-day journey to Moscow on a 'sleeper' train. The remaining 4735 mile journey from Moscow to Beijing took a further 6 days, travelling through Siberia, Mongolia and across the Gobi desert. The trains looked quite comfortable, having private cabins with showers, and seats that converted to beds for sleeping.

Izzy began to daydream about all the sights she might see. Beijing might be over 5000 miles away, but in her mind she was already there.

Where are the 2012 Olympics going to be held?

Where will the 2012 Olympic Games be held? Izzy, Ralph, Max and Spotless disagree. Follow the lines to see which city they think will win.

• TOP TIPS •

To plan a journey anywhere in the world you can't go wrong with www.multimap.com.

It has a fantastic range of maps at different scales for most countries in the world and will even give you detailed travel directions to anywhere in Europe.

DID YOU KNOW?

China has budgeted to spend £20 billion to prepare for, and to host, the Olympic Games in 2008. However, not everybody is happy about the decision to award the Games to Beijing. China has a poor human rights record, but the hope is that the Olympics will improve China's image and help it move towards democracy.

Test your knowledge 9

1 Answer the following questions.

    a) When were the first modern Olympic Games held?

    ....

    b) How many countries competed in the ancient Olympic Games?

    ....

    c) How many countries took part in the first modern Olympic Games?

    ....

    d) Where will the 2012 Olympic Games be held?

    ....

    e) Approximately how many people watch each Olympic Games on television?

    ....

    f) What does the Olympic symbol of five interlocking rings represent?

    ....

(6 marks)

2 Cross out the incorrect words in the sentences below.

    a) The ancient Olympic Games were held in *Greece / Italy*.

    b) The first modern Olympic Games were held in *Spain / Greece* in 1896.

    c) The 2004 Olympic Games were held in *Greece / France*.

    d) The 2008 Olympic Games will be held in *Greece / China*.

    e) There have been *twenty-six / thirty-four* summer Olympic Games since 1896.

    f) The founder of the modern Olympics believed the most important thing was to *win / take part*.

(6 marks)

3 Which of the following factors do the International Olympic Committee consider when deciding where to hold the Olympics?

Factors considered	Yes	No
Amount of funding available		
Average life expectancy		
Public opinion		
Existing sports facilities		
National anthem		
Quality of roads and railways		
Number of fast food restaurants		
Number of hotels		
Impact on the environment		
Number of shops		

(10 marks)

4 Draw a circle around the cities that have hosted the Olympics.

Tokyo   Manchester   Delhi   Mexico City

Moscow   Los Angeles   Nairobi   Barcelona

Sydney   New York

(7 marks)

5 Draw lines to show which of the following are benefits of hosting the Olympic Games.

Raises country's profile
Cost of maintaining buildings
Winning gold medals
Attracts tourists
Money from ticket sales
Increased air pollution
Income from TV companies
Debts to pay for facilities
Money from sponsorship deals
Environmental improvements

Benefit

(5 marks)

6 Arrange the following places in the correct order visited by the Trans-Siberian Railway.

Beijing   Moscow   London   Ulan Bator   Brussels

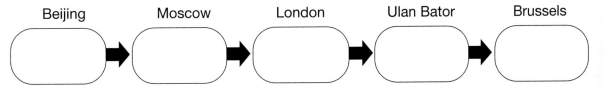

(5 marks)

(Total 39 marks)

Glossary

Active volcano A volcano which has erupted recently and is expected to erupt again in the future.

Atlas A book containing maps and often graphs and tables of data.

Avalanche A mass of snow, ice or rock sliding rapidly down a slope.

Birth control The prevention of pregnancy.

Birth rate The number of live births per thousand people per year.

British Isles The British Isles includes England, Scotland, Wales, Northern Ireland, the Republic of Ireland, the Isle of Man and the Channel Islands

Brownfield land An area of wasteland in a town or city which has previously been built on.

Central Business District The area in a town or city that contains shops, services and offices.

Climate The average weather conditions of a place over a period of at least 30 years.

Cold front The boundary between a mass of cool air beneath and behind a mass of warm air in a low pressure weather system.

Continent A very large continuous expanse of land (Asia, Australia, Africa, Europe, North America, South America, and Antarctica).

Cyclone A tropical storm with powerful winds and very heavy rainfall.

Dam A barrier built across a river to hold back water and form a reservoir.

Death rate The number of deaths per thousand people per year.

Deforestation The large-scale destruction of an area of forest.

Degree The unit used to measure longitude and latitude.

Delta An area of low-lying land at the mouth of a river formed as a result of deposition.

Democracy A form of government in which the people have a voice in the exercise of power.

Detached Describes a house that is not attached to any other houses.

Earthquake Shockwaves caused as energy is released by sudden movements of rock beneath the Earth's surface.

Eastings The grid lines which run north–south on a map.

Embankment A raised bank along the side of a river.

Environment Our surroundings, including the built environment and the natural world.

Erosion The wearing away of the land by wind, water and ice.

Europe This is one of the seven continents.

European Union An organisation for economic and political co-operation between 25 European countries.

Flood An overflow of a large amount of water onto an area that is usually dry.

Floodplain The area of flat land on either side of a river.

Four-figure grid reference Four numbers used to locate a position on an Ordnance Survey map.

Global climate change A gradual change in the Earth's climate, which may be caused by an increase in greenhouse gases in the atmosphere.

Great Britain Great Britain includes England, Scotland and Wales.

Greenfield land An area of land which has not previously been built on.

Greenwich Meridian The zero line of longitude.

Hard engineering
Flood control methods such as dams and embankments.

Human rights Rights which are believed to belong to every person.

Hurricane A tropical storm with powerful winds and very heavy rainfall.

Immigrant A person who moves into a country as a permanent resident.

Impermeable Describes rock which does not allow water to pass through it.

Infrastructure The basic systems and services of a place, such as water supply, electricity, transport and schools.

Landslide A sudden and rapid movement of soil and rock down a slope.

Latitude The position of a place north or south of the equator, measured in degrees from 0° to 90°.

Longitude The position of a place east or west of the Greenwich meridian, measured in degrees from 0° to 180°.

Meander A winding bend or curve in a river.

Migrant A person who moves from one area to another for a particular period of time.

Migration The movement of people from one area to another. Migration may be temporary, seasonal or permanent.

Northings The grid lines which run east–west on a map.

Ordnance Survey The organisation responsible for producing detailed maps of the United Kingdom.

Perception Our beliefs, opinions and way of understanding things – the 'way we see the world'.

Physical geography The study of the natural processes and landforms of the Earth.

Population distribution The way in which people are spread out across an area or country.

Population explosion The rapid increase in global population over the past 200 years.

Reservoir A large lake formed behind a dam.

Scale The scale of a map is the ratio of the drawn distance to its true value.

Semi-detached Describes a house which is attached to another house on one side only.

Six-figure grid references Six numbers used to locate a position on an Ordnance Survey map.

Soft engineering Flood control methods such as planting trees and zoning (banning house-building in high risk areas).

Stereotype An over-simplified and fixed impression about people, places and things.

Terraced Describes a house which is attached to other houses on both sides.

Tornado A powerful rotating column of air.

Tsunami A very large sea wave, usually caused by an earthquake.

United Kingdom The United Kingdom includes England, Scotland, Wales and Northern Ireland.

Volcano An opening in the Earth's crust through which lava, gas, ash and steam are erupted.

Warm front The boundary between a mass of cool air and a mass of warm air below it in a low pressure weather system.

Answers

Your place in the universe p5
Your name; Your house number or name; Your street; Your village, town or city; Your county; Your country; Great Britain; United Kingdom; British Isles; Europe; The world; The universe

The great cycle race p7
Start = London, City 1 = Bristol, City 2 = Cardiff, City 3 = Liverpool, City 4 = Dublin, City 5 = Belfast, City 6 = Glasgow, City 7 = Edinburgh, City 8 = Newcastle, City 9 = Leeds, City 10 = Sheffield, City 11 = Manchester, City 12 = Birmingham

The confused tourist p9
Mountains in England = Pennines, The highest mountain in England = Scafell Pike, Mountains in Wales = Cambrian Mountains, The highest mountain in Wales = Snowdon, Mountains in Scotland = Grampian Mountains, The highest mountain in Scotland = Ben Nevis, The length of the River Thames = 215 miles, The length of the River Trent = 170 miles, The length of the River Severn = 220 miles, The most northerly point = John O'Groats, The most southerly point = Land's End

Project fun p13
1 computer   2 video/notes   3 books   4 notes/video
5 library   6 Internet   7 search engine   8 photographs
Hidden word = RESEARCH

Name that country! p15
a) China   b) Japan   c) UK   d) Italy   e) USA   f) India
g) Australia

World cruise p17
Final destination = Los Angeles, USA

Crack the code p21
The snow falls heavily in Moscow.

Dot to dot p23
Spotless

Yo ho ho ho! A pirate's life for me p25
The treasure is in the mountains.

True or false? p29
The following are all true reasons why we need to build more houses: People are leaving home at a younger age, People are living longer, People are getting married at an older age, More marriages are ending in divorce, People are migrating to other parts of the country

Real or fake? p31
Real: Barton in the Beans, Brown Willy, World's End, Ugley, Little Snoring, Nasty
Fake: Top Wallop, Deadhorse, Little Boring, Belchertown

In the zone p33

It's not just cricket! p37
All the photographs were taken in England

Where are all the people from? p39

Migration puzzle p41
a) France   b) Kenya   c) Mexico   d) Thailand   e) Brazil
f) Spain

Counting pennies p45
The answer is 536 870 912 or £5 368 709.

Population clock p47
Second	4
Minute	240
Hour	142 400
Day	345 600
Month	10 713 600
Year	128 563 200

The number of babies born each year is 128 563 200.
The number of people who die each year is 57 317 760.

The perfect holiday p49
Crowded: A, C, E, G, I
Very few people: B, D, F, H, J

Odd ones out p53
Effects of flooding: Carpets ruined, People evacuated, Cars damaged, Transport difficult, Sewage contamination, Power cuts
Not effects of flooding: Heavy rainfall, Thunderstorm, River bursts banks, Snow melting

Flood crossword p55
Across
5. Billion
6. Rain
7. Thunderstorm
8. Banks
9. Urban
10. Environment

Down
1. Million
2. Impermeable
3. Floodplain
4. Silt

Scrambled words p57
1. Plant trees
2. Reservoir
3. Embankment
4. Dam
5. Floating houses
6. Zoning
7. Widening
8. Deepening
9. Door guard
10. Straightening

Flooding wordsearch p61

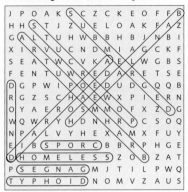

Kriss Kross p63

Across
2. Silt
4. Deforestation
7. Summer

Down
1. Himalayas
2. Storm surge
3. Monsoon
5. Sea level
6. Ganges

Hazard word ladder p65

1 Flood 2 Hurricane 3 Tsunami 4 Volcano
5 Forest fire 6 Tornado 7 Avalanche 8 Earthquake
Hidden word = DISASTER

Name the Olympic dates p69

A = Tokyo (1964), B = Mexico City (1968), C = Munich (1972),
D = Montreal (1976), E = Moscow (1980), F = Los Angeles
(1984), G = Seoul (1988), H = Barcelona (1992),
I = Atlanta (1996), J = Sydney (2000), K = Athens (2004)

The top ten p71

a) USA, b) China, c) Russia, d) Australia, e) Japan,
f) Germany, g) France, h)Italy, i) South Korea, j) Great Britain

Where are the 2012 Olympics going to be held? p73

Izzy picked New York. Ralph picked London. Max picked Paris.
Spotless picked Moscow. Ralph is right.

Test your knowledge 1

1 A = Great Britain, B = United Kingdom, C = British Isles,
   D = England
2 A = London, B = Cardiff, C = Bristol, D = Dublin,
   E = Belfast, F = Glasgow, G = Edinburgh, H = Newcastle,
   I = Leeds, J = Manchester, K = Liverpool, L = Birmingham
3 London, Birmingham, Leeds, Glasgow, Sheffield, Bradford,
   Liverpool, Edinburgh, Manchester, Bristol
4 The countries not in the EU are:
   a) Switzerland b) Russia c) Turkey d) Iceland
   e) Egypt
5 a) False b) True c) True d) False e) False f) True
   g) True h) False

Test your knowledge 2

1 a) Library b) Notes c) Internet d) Computer e) Book
   f) Photographs g) Video h) Search engine
2 A = China, B = India, C = UK, D = USA, E = Japan,
   F = Italy, G = Australia
3 A = North Pole, B = Tropic of Cancer, C = Equator,
   D = Tropic of Capricorn, E = South Pole, F = Greenwich
   Meridian
4 a) North America b) Asia c) Europe d) Antarctica
   e) South America f) Australia g) Africa

Test your knowledge 3

1 a) Middleton   b) Great Waldingfield c) Ballingdon
2 a) 86 45   b) 92 45   c) 89 44
3 a) Church with a tower

   b) Campsite

   c) Public telephone

4 a)   877 411

   b)   916 405

   c) PH   893 453

5 a) North   b) West   c) South east
6 a) 3.2 km   b) 5.2 km c) 4.8 km

Test your knowledge 4

1 a) Greenfield land is land which has not been built on
      before.
   b) Brownfield land is land which has been built on
      previously.
   c) 4.4 million
   d) 60%
   e) 10 000 years ago
   f) A city with a population of over 10 million
2 a) People are *leaving* home at a younger age.
   b) The population is *increasing*.
   c) People are *living* longer.
   d) People are getting *married* at an older age.
   e) People are *divorcing* more frequently.
   f) People are *migrating* to other parts of the country.
3 burg = fortified dwelling by = homestead
   thorpe = a new village   thwaite = meadow
   ton = farming village
4 The high land is good for defence and has building
   materials (timber and stone), fuel (timber), sites safe from
   flooding, and a water supply. The flat land is good for
   building and has fertile soil for farming (floodplain), and is
   close to a road.
5 Mixture of shops, offices and leisure facilities = Central
   Business District (CBD)
   Attached to other houses on both sides = Terraced houses
   Attached to another house on one side = Semi-detached
   houses
   Not attached to any other houses = Detached houses

Test your knowledge 5

1 a) 'Perception' means our beliefs, opinions and way of
      understanding things.
   b) A 'stereotype' is an over-simplified, and fixed
      impression about people, places and things.
   c) 'Migration' is the movement of people from one place to
      another, often between countries.
   d) An 'immigrant' is a person who moves to another
      country permanently.
   e) 92.1%
   f) 500 000
   g) 350 000
2 Fish and chips = England, Pizza = Italy, Burger = USA, Bowl
   of rice = China, Baguette = France, Big sausage = Germany,
   Taco = Mexico, Sushi = Japan

3 Romans, Saxons, Vikings, Normans, West Indians, Indians, Pakistanis, Bangladeshis
4 Push factors = natural disasters, wars, drought, unemployment
Pull factors = good hospitals, free education, well-paid jobs, good weather

Test your knowledge 6

1 a) The term 'population explosion' means the rapid growth in global population since 1800.
  b) It was caused by improvements in standards of living which reduced death rates whilst birth rates remained stable.
  c) China has limited the number of babies to a maximum of one per woman.
  d) Monaco
  e) 6.5 billion
2 Our earliest ancestors were ape-like creatures that lived about *four* million years ago. It was not until *one* hundred thousand years ago that 'homo sapiens' evolved in East Africa. Gradually, human beings spread out from Africa to *Europe*, across to Asia, down to *Australia*, into North *America* and finally into South America. *Two* thousand years ago there were only about *three* hundred million people on the planet, but by 1800 the population reached one *billion*. This number doubled to two billion by 1923, and reached *six* billion in 1999. It is predicted that the global population will peak at over *ten* billion in 2200.
3 a) False b) True c) True d) False e) True f) False
4 Global population increase per day is 191 520.
5 a) Positive b) Positive c) Negative d) Positive
  e) Positive f) Negative g) Negative h) Negative

Test your knowledge 7

1 a) The Environment Agency
  b) A flash flood is a sudden and severe flood that can cause a huge amount of damage very quickly.
  c) Flash floods are most likely in urban areas where the ground is impermeable, or in areas such as deserts where the ground has been baked hard.
  d) 2 million
  e) £1 billion
  f) Methods such as dams and embankments are known as hard engineering. Methods such as planting trees, and zoning are known as 'soft engineering'.
2 Sensible things to do: Move furniture upstairs, Turn off the electricity, Pile sandbags in front of doors, Evacuate the area, Take up carpets
Daft things to do: Take your canoe for a paddle, Go swimming, Dig a moat around your house, Call the coastguard, Put sticky tape around your doors and windows
3 Effects of flooding include: possessions ruined, people evacuated, cars damaged, transport difficult, sewage contamination, power cuts
4 Genuine causes of flooding are: b) A long period of rainfall, c) A thunderstorm during the summer, e) Impermeable rock such as clay, f) Snow melt in spring, h) Building on the flood plain i) cutting down trees
5 a) Dam b) Deepen c) Embankment d) Straighten
  e) Zoning f) Flood guards

Test your knowledge 8

1 a) The main rivers which cause flooding in Bangladesh are the Ganges, Brahmaputra and Meghna.
  b) Flooding occurs in summer in Bangladesh.
  c) Flooding in a poor country can cause food shortages by destroying crops.
  d) Stagnant water allows mosquitoes to breed.
  e) LEDCs have a poorly developed infrastructure (transport, water supply, electricity supply) and cannot afford to deal with the effects of a major flood.
2 Effects of flooding in Bangladesh: a) Hundreds of deaths, c) Millions of people homeless, d) Crops drowned and ruined, g) Animals drowned, h) Contaminated drinking water, i) Snake bites
3 a) Bangladesh has over *250* rivers.
  b) Many of Bangladesh's rivers begin in the foothills of the *Himalayas*.
  c) Bangladesh receives monsoon rainfall in the *summer*.
  d) Nearly *75%* of Bangladesh is less than one metre above sea level.
  e) When the river floods it deposits *fertile* silt on the floodplain.
  f) Deforestation in *India* may be contributing to flooding in Bangladesh.
  g) Eighty percent of Bangladesh is a river *delta*.
  h) Tropical cyclones can cause the sea to rise by up to *five* metres.
4 a) Flood b) Hurricane c) Tornado d) Earthquake
  e) Landslide f) Tsunami g) Avalanche h) Volcano
5 Most dangerous → Asia → Caribbean and Central America → Europe → Africa → North America → Australia → Least dangerous

Test your knowledge 9

1 a) The first modern Olympic Games were held in 1896.
  b) Only Greek athletes competed in the ancient Olympics.
  c) Fourteen countries took part in the first modern Olympics.
  d) The 2012 Olympics will be in London.
  e) Three billion people watch each Olympic Games on television.
  f) The rings represent the five continents of the Americas, Europe, Asia, Africa and Oceania.
2 a) The ancient Olympic Games were held in *Greece*.
  b) The first modern Olympic Games were held in *Greece* in 1896.
  c) The 2004 Olympic Games were held in *Greece*.
  d) The 2008 Olympic Games will be held in *China*.
  e) There have been *twenty-six* summer Olympic Games since 1896.
  f) The founder of the modern Olympics believed the most important thing was to *take part*.
3 Factors considered are: Amount of funding available, Public opinion, Existing sports facilities, Quality of roads and railways, Number of hotels, Impact on the environment
4 Cities that have hosted the Games: Tokyo, Mexico City, Moscow, Los Angeles, Barcelona, Sydney
5 Benefits of hosting the Olympic Games: Raises country's profile, Attracts tourists, Money from ticket sales, Income from TV companies, Money from sponsorship deals, Environmental improvements
6 London → Brussels → Moscow → Ulan Bator → Beijing